P9-CFS-650

AP® MACROECONOMICS
CRASH COURSE®

Jason Welker, M.Ed.

Research & Education Association
Visit our website at: www.rea.com

Research & Education Association
61 Ethel Road West
Piscataway, New Jersey 08854
Email: info@rea.com

AP® MACROECONOMICS CRASH COURSE®

Published 2018
Copyright © 2012 by Research & Education Association, Inc.
All rights reserved. No part of this book may be reproduced
in any form without permission of the publisher.

Printed in the United States of America

Library of Congress Control Number 2011931950

ISBN-13: 978-0-7386-0971-3
ISBN-10: 0-7386-0971-4

AP MACROECONOMICS CRASH COURSE TABLE OF CONTENTS

 INTRODUCTION

 BASIC ECONOMIC CONCEPTS

PART III **MEASUREMENT OF ECONOMIC PERFORMANCE**

PART IV

NATIONAL INCOME AND PRICE DETERMINATION

PART V

FINANCIAL SECTOR

PART VI

MACROECONOMIC POLICIES, INFLATION, AND UNEMPLOYMENT

PART VII

ECONOMIC GROWTH AND PRODUCTIVITY

ABOUT OUR AUTHOR

Jason Welker's interest in economics began in the late 1990s, when, as a high school student studying economics at an international school in Malaysia, he experienced firsthand the effects of the Asian financial crisis that saw the economies of Southeast Asia plunge into recession and trigger widespread political unrest. At university in Seattle, Jason once again witnessed the power that economics holds over society when the World Trade Organization's Seattle summit attracted tens of thousands of protesters, whose anger over globalization escalated into riots. From these experiences, and with the inspiration provided by his Intro to Economics professors, Jason decided he wanted to dedicate his studies to understanding the role economics plays in shaping human societies. His personal economics education has continued ever since.

Jason's international teaching career has taken him to schools in Thailand, China, and most recently to Switzerland, where he taught Advanced Placement and International Baccalaureate Economics at an international school in Zurich, the financial capital of Europe.

In addition to teaching economics to nearly 100 students from 40 countries each year, Jason writes a blog for Economics students around the world which can be read at *www.welkerswikinomics.com*. He has also led workshops on technology in the Economics classroom at AP Summer Institutes and at the National Center for Economics Education conference in Washington, D.C. He has recently completed a textbook for the IB Economics curriculum, and is constantly developing and making available many other resources for Econ students through his website. His latest venture, *AP Macroeconomics Crash Course*, provides students with a powerful resource for use in preparation for their AP exams.

ABOUT OUR BOOK

REA's *AP Macroeconomics Crash Course* is designed for the last-minute studier or any student who wants a quick refresher on the AP course. The *Crash Course* is based on the latest changes to the AP Macroeconomics course and exam and focuses only on the topics tested, so you can make the most of your study time.

Written by a veteran AP Macroeconomics test expert, our *Crash Course* gives you a concise review of the major concepts and important topics tested on the AP Macroeconomics exam.

- **Part I** offers you our **Keys for Success**, so you can tackle the exam with confidence. It also gives you **Key Formulas and Definitions** that you must know.

- **Parts II through VIII** review all of the topics found on the exam, including **Basic Economic Concepts**, the **Financial Sector**, **Economic Growth**, and **International Trade and Finance**, among others.

- **Part IX** offers specific **Test-Taking Strategies** for both the multiple-choice questions and the free-response questions.

- Finally, a **Glossary of Economics Terms** is included that defines the most important economics terms or concepts you need to understand in AP Macroeconomics.

ABOUT OUR ONLINE PRACTICE TEST

How ready are you for the AP Macroeconomics exam? Find out by taking **REA's online practice exam** available at *www.rea.com/studycenter*. This test features automatic scoring, detailed explanations of all answers, and diagnostic score reporting that will help you identify your strengths and weaknesses so you'll be ready on exam day.

Whether you use this book throughout the school year or as a refresher in the final weeks before the exam, REA's *Crash Course* will show you how to study efficiently and strategically, so you can boost your score.

Good luck on your AP Macroeconomics exam!

ACKNOWLEDGMENTS

In addition to our author, we would like to thank Larry B. Kling, Vice President, Editorial, for his overall guidance; Pam Weston, Publisher, for setting the quality standards for production integrity and managing the publication to completion; John Cording, Vice President, Technology, for coordinating the design and development of the REA Study Center; and Diane Goldschmidt, Senior Editor, for editorial project management.

We would also like to extend special thanks to Tyson Smith of Iowa City West High School for technically reviewing the manuscript, Elizabeth Catafalmo for copyediting, Caroline Duffy for proofreading, and Kathy Caratozzolo of Caragraphics for typesetting this edition.

PART I
INTRODUCTION

Keys for Success
on the AP Macroeconomics Exam

The subject of macroeconomics is vast in content and at the university level it may be taught over the span of several years of courses. In fact, one could even major in a macroeconomic topic and pursue advanced degrees within the field. You, on the other hand, are probably taking AP Macroeconomics as a one- or possibly two-semester high school course in the 11th or 12th grade.

So how can a high school student be expected to learn all the content that may be considered macroeconomics and be prepared enough to score a respectable mark on the Advanced Placement exam? Rest assured, with a few crucial pieces of information and some important hints and tips, you can focus your studies in and out of the classroom toward the *most* important concepts that are *most* likely to be addressed on the AP Macro exam.

This *Crash Course*, along with your course textbook, your teacher, your classmates and countless online resources, is your single greatest key to success on the AP Macro exam. There is no shortage of resources in print and online for the high school economics student today.

RELATIVE IMPORTANCE OF THE AP MACRO UNITS ON THE EXAM

With all the information out there, how do you know in what areas to *focus*? One thing all AP Macro students should know as they progress through the course and prepare for the exam is the relative importance of each of the units in the course.

The AP Macro exam is a two-part examination. The first part is a 60-question multiple-choice (MC) test. The 60 questions come from the seven units of the AP Macro course. Thankfully, the College Board publishes the approximate percentage of the 60 multiple-choice questions that will come from each of the seven sections of the course. The breakdown is as follows:

> ➤ Unit 1: Basic Economic Concepts, Supply, Demand, and Equilibrium (8–12 percent)

> ➤ Unit 2: Measurement of Economic Performance (12–16 percent)

> ➤ Unit 3: National Income and Price Determination (10–15 percent)

> ➤ Unit 4: The Financial Sector (15–20 percent)

> ➤ Unit 5: Macroeconomic Policies, Inflation, and Unemployment (20–30 percent)

> ➤ Unit 6: Economic Growth and Productivity (5–10 percent)

> ➤ Unit 7: Open Economy: International Trade and Finance (10–15 percent)

With the approximate percentages of each unit's representation on the multiple-choice section of the exam, you can focus your exam studies appropriately. For example, as shown above, the most commonly tested units are Unit 4—The Financial Sector, and Unit 5—Macroeconomic Policies. These two units together could make up as much as 50 percent of the 60 questions on the multiple-choice section of the exam.

As you use this *Crash Course* to study, you will notice that the most heavily assessed units are given the most attention in this book. Units 4 and 5, for example, account for more than 60 pages. In this way, the number of pages dedicated to each unit in the *Crash Course* is roughly representative of the weight that unit is given on the AP exam.

The free-response question (FRQ) section of the exam includes three questions. The first question is always a long FRQ, on which you are expected to spend approximately 30 minutes planning and answering. The second and third questions are short FRQs, on which you are expected to spend approximately 15 minutes planning and answering. The topics the FRQs cover could come from any section of the syllabus, although there are certain topics that are more commonly tested than others, giving the FRQ section some degree of predictability. The last two chapters of this *Crash Course* provide more information about how to best prepare for these two sections of the AP exam.

GRADE SCALE FOR THE AP MACRO EXAM

You may think with all the units in this course and only one or two semesters to learn them all, you'll never be able to get a 5 on the AP Macroeconomics exam. However, getting a 4 or 5 on the exam may not be as difficult as you might think. The table below shows the approximate range of scores needed to earn each of the possible AP scores, from the top mark of 5 to the lowest score of 1.

Keep in mind that the exam includes a 60-question multiple-choice section and a 3-question free-response section. The free-response questions will always be weighted so that the long question is worth half the free-response points and the short questions will each be worth a quarter of the free-response points. The multiple-choice section is worth twice as much as the free-response portion. In addition, the exact range of each of the five possible grades will vary depending upon how students who took the exam perform. But usually, the range of scores is as follows:

AP Grade	Minimum Percentage Correct on MC and FRQ Sections Combined
5	81%
4	62%
3	48%
2	33%
1	0%

The score ranges indicated above are only an approximation. The precise score range is adjusted every year based on the performance of students worldwide on that year's exam.

WHEN TO GUESS IN THE MULTIPLE-CHOICE SECTION

Students often wonder, "If I have no idea which of the five options is correct, should I guess?" Yes, guessing is advised if, of course, you have no idea of the correct answer. Before resorting to a blind guess, however, you should use all your knowledge and understanding of economics to eliminate the possible incorrect answers, so that any guess you are forced to make is an *educated guess.*

USING SUPPLEMENTARY MATERIALS

This *Crash Course* contains everything you need to know to score well on the AP exam. You should, however, supplement it with the notes you took in class, your textbook, and materials available from the College Board (*www.collegeboard.org*).

The website you should bookmark and use frequently throughout the AP Macro course, especially when preparing for the exam, is the College Board's site for AP Macroeconomics students (*www.collegeboard.org/apcourses*).

This site includes the following:

➤ Sample free-response questions and scoring guidelines

➤ Official topic outline

➤ Exam information

➤ A link to the course description, which includes sample multiple-choice questions

In addition to that material, REA's *AP Microeconomics & Macroeconomics All Access* Book + Web + Mobile study system further enhances your exam preparation by offering a comprehensive review book plus a suite of online assessments (end-of-chapter quizzes, mini-tests, a full-length practice test, and e-flashcards), all designed to pinpoint your strengths and weaknesses and help focus your study for the exam.

THE IMPORTANCE OF DIAGRAMS IN THE AP MACRO COURSE

To earn a 4 or 5 on the AP Macro exam, you must possess more than just a solid understanding of the course material. You also must be skilled at illustrating the concepts from the course in detailed, correctly drawn economics diagrams.

The good news is that all the graphs you need to know are drawn exactly as they should be drawn in the exam right here in this *Crash Course*. Study these diagrams closely as you progress through this book. Examine the labels, the shapes of the lines, the way arrows are used to indicate directions of shifts, and the way dotted lines are used to identify equilibrium points on the axes. Seek to understand the meaning of the various macroeconomic models in this book, and don't just memorize them.

Drawing graphs well (and being able to interpret their meaning in the MC section) is a crucial skill that will ensure you impress the examiners who read your free-response answers. Each line on a graph should be seen as telling a story—a relationship between the variables on the axes of that particular graph. If you strive for understanding why each line is shaped as it is, of what it is composed, and which factors can shift it, you will perform well on graph-based questions whether you encounter them in the MC or free-response section of the test.

USING THE *AP MACROECONOMICS CRASH COURSE* TO PREPARE FOR SUCCESS

This *Crash Course* has been written based on careful analysis of the AP Macroeconomics Course Description and on past multiple-choice and free-response questions. Chapter 2 contains key formulas and definitions that you absolutely *need to know*. Chapters 3–17 provide you with a detailed examination of each of the topics from the AP Macro syllabus, in the same order as the syllabus itself. Along with written explanations, these chapters include precisely drawn diagrams. Study these diagrams closely, and as you prepare for the exam, practice drawing all the graphs you see in this book on your own.

The *Crash Course* is a detailed *outline* of the course, but does not go into great depth or provide many examples of the theories and concepts covered. You should depend on your teacher, your class-mates, textbooks, and online resources for that information. Use this book in the last few weeks before the big exam to supplement the learning you do elsewhere.

Key Formulas and Definitions
for AP Macroeconomics

I. Key Formulas

1. GDP = C + I + G + Xn: The expenditure approach to measuring GDP correlates well with aggregate demand (AD).

2. GDP = W + I + R + P: The income approach to measuring GDP correlates well with aggregate supply (AS).

3. Calculating Nominal GDP: The quantity of various goods produced in a nation times their current prices, added together.

4. GDP Deflator: A price index used to adjust nominal GDP to arrive at real GDP. Called the "deflator" because nominal GDP will usually overstate the value of a nation's output if there has been inflation. The Consumer Price Index (CPI) is another commonly used price index.

5. Real GDP: $\dfrac{\text{Nominal GDP}}{\text{GDP deflator}} \times 100$.

6. GDP Growth Rate:
$\dfrac{\text{Current year's GDP} - \text{Last year's GDP}}{\text{Last year's GDP}} \times 100$. The GDP growth rate is a percentage change in a nation's real output between one year and the next.

7. The Inflation Rate via the CPI:
$\dfrac{\text{This year's CPI} - \text{Last year's CPI}}{\text{Last year's CPI}} \times 100$. The inflation rate is the percentage change in the CPI from one period to the next.

8. Real Interest Rate = nominal interest rate − inflation rate.

9. Unemployment Rate = $\dfrac{\text{Number of unemployed}}{\text{Number in the labor force}} \times 100$. The labor force includes all non-institutionalized people of working age who are employed or seeking employment.

10. Money Multiplier = $\dfrac{1}{\text{RRR}}$ where RRR equals the required reserve ratio. Application: An initial injection of $1,000 of new money into a banking system with a reserve ratio of 0.1 will generate up to $1,000 × (10) = $10,000 in total money.

11. Quantity Theory of Money: MV = PQ = Y. A monetarist's view that explains how changes in the money supply (M) will affect the price level (P) and/or real output assuming the velocity of money (V) is fixed in the short run.

12. MPC + MPS = 1. The fraction of an increase in disposable income that is spent (MPC) plus the fraction that is saved (MPS) must equal 1.

13. Spending Multiplier = $\dfrac{1}{1-\text{MPC}}$ or $\dfrac{1}{\text{MPS}}$. This tells you how much total spending an initial injection of spending in the economy will generate. For example, if the MPC = .8 and the government spends $100 million, then the total increase in spending in the economy = $100 × 5 = $500 million.

14. Tax Multiplier = $\dfrac{-\text{MPC}}{\text{MPS}}$. This tells you how much total spending will result from an initial change in the level of taxation. It is negative because when taxes decrease, spending increases, and vice versa. The tax multiplier will always be smaller than the spending multiplier.

II. Key Definitions

1. Absolute Advantage: A country or individual has an absolute advantage in the production of a good when the country can produce the good using fewer resources than another country or individual.

2. Aggregate Demand (AD): A schedule or curve that shows the total quantity demand for all goods and services of a nation at various price levels at a given period of time.

3. Aggregate Supply (AS): The total amount of goods and services that all the firms in all the industries in a country will produce at various price levels in a given period of time.

4. Appreciation: An increase in the value of one currency relative to another, resulting from an increase in demand for or a decrease in supply of the currency on the foreign exchange market.

5. Balance of Payments: Measures all the monetary exchanges between one nation and all other nations. Includes the current account and the capital account.

6. Bonds: A certificate of debt issued by a company or a government to an investor.

7. Budget Deficit: When a government spends more than it collects in tax revenues in a given year.

8. Business Cycle: A model showing the short-run periods of contraction and expansion in output experienced by an economy over a period of time.

9. Capital: Human-made resources (machinery and equipment) used to produce goods and services; goods that do not directly satisfy human wants. Sometimes separated into human capital (education, know-how) and physical capital (tools you can touch and operate).

10. Capital Account (also called the Financial Account): Measures the flow of funds for investment in real assets (such as factories or office buildings) or financial assets (such as stocks and bonds) between a nation and the rest of the world.

11. *Ceteris Paribus*: "Other things being equal;" used as a reminder that all variables other than the ones being studied are assumed to be constant.

12. Circular Flow Diagram: A model of the macroeconomy that shows the interconnectedness of businesses, households, government, banks, and the foreign sectors. Money flows in

a circular direction, and goods, services, and resources flow in the opposite direction.

13. Classical Economic Theory: The view that an economy will self-correct from periods of economic shock if left alone. Also known as "laissez-faire."

14. Comparative Advantage: When an individual, a firm or a nation is able to produce a particular product at a lower-opportunity cost than another individual, firm, or nation. Comparative advantage is the basis on which nations trade with one another.

15. Consumer Price Index (CPI): An index that measures the price of a fixed market basket of consumer goods bought by a typical consumer. The CPI is used to calculate the inflation rate in a nation.

16. Consumption: A component of a nation's aggregate demand; measures the total spending by domestic households on goods and services.

17. Contractionary Fiscal Policy: A demand-side policy whereby government increases taxes or decreases its expenditures in order to reduce aggregate demand. Could be used in a period of high inflation to bring down the inflation rate.

18. Contractionary Monetary Policy: A demand-side policy whereby the central bank reduces the supply of money, increasing interest rates and reducing aggregate demand. Could be used to bring down high inflation rates.

19. Cost-Push Inflation: Inflation resulting from a decrease in AS (from higher wage rates and raw material prices, such as the price of oil) and accompanied by a decrease in real output and employment. Also referred to as "stagflation" or "adverse aggregate supply shock."

20. Crowding-Out Effect: The rise in interest rates and the resulting decrease in investment spending in the economy caused by increased government borrowing in the loanable funds market. Seen as a disadvantageous side effect of expansionary fiscal policy.

21. Current Account: Measures the balance of trade in goods and services and the flow of income between one nation

and all other nations. It also records monetary gifts or grants that flow into or out of a country. Equal to a country's *net* exports, or its exports minus its imports.

22. Cyclical Unemployment: Unemployment caused by a fall in aggregate demand in a nation. Not included in the natural rate of unemployment. When a nation is in a recession, there will be cyclical unemployment.

23. Deflation: A decrease in the average price level of a nation's output over time.

24. Demand Deposit: A deposit in a commercial bank against which checks may be written. Also known as a "checkable deposit."

25. Demand-Pull Inflation: Inflation resulting from an increase in AD without a corresponding increase in AS.

26. Depreciation: A decrease in the value of one currency relative to another, resulting from a decrease in demand for or an increase in the supply of the currency on the foreign exchange market.

27. Devaluation: When a government intervenes in the market for its own currency to weaken it relative to another currency. Usually achieved through direct intervention in the foreign exchange (forex) market or through the use of monetary policy that affects interest rates, and thereby affects international demand for the currency.

28. Discount Rate: One of the three tools of monetary policy, it is the interest rate that the federal government charges on the loans it makes to commercial banks.

29. Economic Growth: An increase in the potential output of goods and services in a nation over time.

30. Economic Resources: Land, labor, capital, and entrepreneurial ability that are used in the production of goods and services. They are "economic" resources because they are scarce (limited in supply and desired). Also known as "factors of production."

31. Excess Reserves: The amount by which a bank's actual reserves exceed its required reserves. Banks can lend excess

reserves; when they do, they expand the money supply. The amount of excess reserves in the banking system determines equilibrium interest rate.

32. Exchange Rate: The price of one currency in terms of another currency, determined in the forex market.

33. Exports: The spending by foreigners on domestically produced goods and services. Counts as an injection into a nation's circular flow of income.

34. Federal Funds Rate (FFR): The interest rate banks charge one another on overnight loans made out of their excess reserves. The FFR is the interest rate targeted by the Fed through its open-market operations.

35. Fiscal Policy: Changes in government spending and tax collections implemented by government with the aim of either increasing or decreasing aggregate demand to achieve the macroeconomic objectives of full employment and price-level stability.

36. Floating Exchange Rate System: When a currency's exchange rate is determined by the free interaction of supply and demand in international forex markets.

37. Forex Market (Foreign Exchange Market): The market in which international buyers and sellers exchange foreign currencies for one another to buy and sell goods, services, and assets from various countries. It is where a currency's exchange rate relative to other currencies is determined.

38. Fractional Reserve Banking: A banking system in which banks hold only a fraction of deposits as required reserves and can lend some of the money deposited by their customers to other borrowers.

39. Frictional Unemployment: Unemployment of workers who have employable skills, such as those who are voluntarily moving between jobs or recent graduates who are looking for their first job.

40. Full Employment: When an economy is producing at a level of output at which almost all the nation's resources are employed. The unemployment rate when an economy is at

full employment equals the natural rate, and includes only frictional and structural unemployment. Full-employment output is also referred to as "potential output."

41. GDP (Gross Domestic Product): The total market value of all final goods and services produced during a given time period within a country's borders. Equal to the total income of the nation's households or the total expenditures on the nation's output.

42. GDP Deflator: The price index for all final goods and services used to adjust the nominal GDP into real GDP.

43. Human Capital: The value skills integrated into labor through education, training, knowledge, and health. An important determinant of aggregate supply and the level of economic growth in a nation.

44. Imports: Spending on goods and services produced in foreign nations. Counts as a leakage from a nation's circular flow of income.

45. Inflation: A rise in the average level of prices in the economy over time (percentage change in the CPI).

46. Inflationary Gap: The difference between a nation's equilibrium level of output and its full employment level of output when the nation is overheating (producing beyond its full employment level).

47. Inflationary Spiral: The rapid increase in average price level resulting from demand-pull inflation leading to higher wages, causing cost push inflation.

48. Interest Rate: The opportunity cost of money. Either the cost of borrowing money or the cost of spending money (e.g., the interest rate is what would be given up by not saving money). Conversely, this is the price a lender is paid for allowing someone else to use money for a time.

49. Investment: A component of aggregate demand, it includes all spending on capital equipment, inventories, and technology by firms. This does not include financial investment, which is the purchase of financial assets (stocks and bonds). Also includes household purchasing of newly constructed residences.

50. Law of Increasing Opportunity Cost: As more of a particular product is produced, the opportunity cost, in terms of what must be given up of other goods to produce each unit of the product, increases. Explains the convex shape of a nation's production possibilities curve.

51. Loanable Funds Market: The market in which the demand for private investment and the supply of household savings intersect to determine the equilibrium real interest rate.

52. Long Run: The period of time over which the wage rate and price level of inputs in a nation are flexible. In the long run, any changes in AD are cancelled out due to the flexibility of wages and prices and an economy will return to its full employment level of output. Sometimes referred to as the "flexible wage period."

53. Long Run Aggregate Supply (LRAS): The level of output to which an economy will always return in the long run. The LRAS curve intersects the horizontal axis at the full employment or potential level of output.

54. M1: A component of the money supply including currency and checkable deposits.

55. M2: A more broadly defined component of the money supply. Equal to M1 plus savings deposits, money-market deposits, mutual funds, and small-time deposits.

56. M3: The broadest component of the money supply. Equal to M2 plus large time deposits.

57. Macroeconomics: The study of entire nations' economies and the interactions between households, firms, government, and foreigners.

58. Macroeconomic Equilibrium: The level of output at which a nation is producing at any particular period of time. May be below its full employment level (if the economy is in recession) or beyond its full employment level (if the economy is overheating).

59. Managed or Fixed Exchange Rate System: When a government or central bank takes action to manage or fix the value

of its currency relative to another currency on the forex market.

60. Marginal Analysis: Decision-making which involves a comparison of marginal (extra) benefits and marginal costs.

61. Marginal Propensity to Consume (MPC): The fraction of any change in income spent on domestically produced goods and services; equal to the change in consumption divided by the change in disposable income.

62. Marginal Propensity to Save (MPS): The fraction of any change in income that is saved; equal to the change in savings divided by the change in disposable income.

63. Market Economic System: A system of resource allocation in which buyers and sellers meet in markets to determine the price and quantity of goods, services, and productive resources.

64. Microeconomics: The study of the interactions between consumers and producers in markets for individual products.

65. Monetarism: The macroeconomic view that the main cause of changes in aggregate output and the price level are fluctuations in the money supply.

66. Monetary Policy: The central bank's manipulation of the supply of money aimed at raising or lowering interest rates to stimulate or contract the level of aggregate demand to promote the macroeconomic objectives of price-level stability and full employment.

67. Money: Any object that can be used to facilitate the exchange of goods and services in a market.

68. Money Demand: The sum of the transaction demand and the asset demand for money. Inversely related to the nominal interest rate.

69. Money Market: The market where the supply of money is set by the central bank; includes the downward-sloping money-demand curve and a vertical money-supply curve. The "price" of money is the nominal interest rate.

70. Money Supply: The vertical curve representing the total supply of excess reserves in a nation's banking system. Determined by the monetary policy actions of the central bank.

71. Multiplier Effect: The increase in total spending in an economy resulting from an initial injection of new spending. The size of the multiplier effect depends upon the spending multiplier.

72. Natural Rate of Unemployment (NRU): The level of unemployment that prevails in an economy that is producing at its full employment level of output. Includes structural and frictional unemployment. While countries' NRUs can vary, the NRU in the United States tends to be close to 5 percent.

73. Net Exports: A component of aggregate demand that equals the income earned from the sale of exports to the rest of the world minus expenditures by domestic consumers on imports.

74. Official Reserves: To balance the two accounts in the balance of payments (current and financial accounts), a country's official foreign exchange reserves measures the net effect of all the money flows from the other accounts.

75. Open-Market Operations: The central bank's buying and selling of government bonds on the open market from commercial banks and the public. This is aimed at increasing or decreasing the level of reserves in the banking system and thereby affects the interest rate and the level of aggregate demand.

76. Opportunity Cost: What must be given up to have anything else. Opportunity costs are not necessarily monetary costs, but rather include what you could do with the resources you use to undertake any activity or exchange.

77. Phillips Curve (long run): A curve vertical at the natural rate of unemployment showing that in the long run there is no trade-off between the price level and the level of unemployment in an economy.

78. Phillips Curve (short run): A downward-sloping curve showing the short-run inverse relationship between the level of inflation and the level of unemployment.

79. Production Possibilities Curve (PPC): A graph that shows the various combinations of output that the economy can produce given the available factors of production and the available production technology.

80. Productivity: The output per unit of input of a resource. An important determinant of the level of aggregate supply in a nation.

81. Protectionism: The use of tariffs, quotas, or subsidies to give domestic producers a competitive advantage over foreign producers. Meant to protect domestic production and employment from foreign competition.

82. Rational Expectations Theory: The hypothesis that business firms and households expect monetary and fiscal policies to have certain effects on the economy and take, in pursuit of their own self-interests, actions which make these policies ineffective at changing real output.

83. Recession: A contraction in total output of goods and services in a nation between two periods of time. Could be caused by a decrease in aggregate demand or in aggregate supply.

84. Recessionary Gap: The difference between an economy's equilibrium level of output and its full employment level of output when an economy is in recession.

85. Required Reserves: The proportion of a bank's total deposits it is required to keep in reserve with the central bank. Determined by the required reserve ratio.

86. Scarcity: Something is scarce when it is both desired and limited in supply. Scarcity is the basic economic problem.

87. Self-Correction: The idea that an economy producing at an equilibrium level of output that is below or above its full employment will return on its own to its full employment level if left to its own devices. Requires flexible wages and prices and is associated with classical economic views.

88. Stagflation: A macroeconomic situation in which both inflation and unemployment increase. Caused by a negative supply shock.

89. Sticky Wage and Price Model: The short-run Aggregate-Supply Curve is sometimes referred to as the "sticky wage and price model," because workers' wage demands take time to adjust to changes in the overall price level, and therefore, in the short run an economy may produce well below or beyond its full employment level of output.

90. Structural Unemployment: Unemployment caused by changes in the structure of demand for goods and in technology; workers who are unemployed because they do not match what is in demand by producers in the economy or whose skills have been left behind by economic advancement.

91. Supply Shock: Anything that leads to a sudden, unexpected change in aggregate supply. Can be negative (decreases AS) or positive (increases AS). May include a change in energy prices, wages, or business taxes, or may result from a natural disaster or a new discovery of important resources.

92. Trade Deficit: When a country's total spending on imported goods and services exceeds its total revenues from the sale of exports to the rest of the world. Synonymous with a deficit in the current account of the balance of payments and with a negative net export component of GDP.

93. Trade Surplus: When a country's sale of exports exceeds its spending on imports. Synonymous with a surplus in the current account of the balance of payments.

94. Wealth: An important determinant of consumption. Wealth is the total value of a household's assets minus all its liabilities.

PART II
BASIC ECONOMIC CONCEPTS

Basic Economic Concepts

I. What is Economics?

A. Definition of Economics

1. *Economics* is the social science that deals with the problem of how to allocate the world's scarce resources between the competing and unlimited wants and needs of people.

2. A *social science* is a field of academic scholarship that examines the interactions, between humans, our institutions, our organizations, and the natural and social environment we inhabit.

B. Definition of Scarcity

1. Something is scarce when it is both desired and limited.

   i. Diamonds are scarce because they are desired and extremely limited.

   ii. Air is not scarce because it is desired but not limited.

   iii. Malaria is not scarce because it is limited but not desired.

   iv. Resources are scarce because they are desired to produce the goods and services society demands but are available in limited quantities.

C. The Basic Economic Problem

1. Humans' wants and needs are infinite, but the resources needed to satisfy these wants and needs are limited and scarce.

2. Because of scarcity, people face choices and need to sacrifice something when they want more of something else. There is a need for the field of study called "economics" because people naturally wish to have as much of what they want as possible. The economic problem is how to best allocate scarce resources to meet the wants and needs of human societies.

3. The scarce resources are the factors of production needed to produce any good or service humans may want or need.

   i.   Land Resources. *Land resources* are those things that are "gifts of nature." Soil, wood, oil, gas, minerals, and animals are all scarce because they are desired to produce goods and services but limited in nature.

   ii. Labor Resources. *Labor* refers to the human resources used in the production of goods and services. Some types of labor are scarcer than others. Factory workers are desirable in huge numbers in many parts of the world, but they are not very limited in places like China and India; therefore, they are not relatively scarce. Medical doctors are desired in all parts of the world, yet they are far more limited in number than people who are able to work in factories; therefore, doctors are relatively scarce.

   iii. Capital Resources. *Capital* refers to the tools and technologies that are used to produce the goods and services we desire. Since more and better tools enhance the production of all types of goods and services (from cars to computers to education to haircuts) but the amount of capital in the world is limited, capital is a scarce resource.

   iv. Entrepreneurship. *Entrepreneurship* is the innovation and creativity applied in the production of goods and services. The physical scarcity of land, labor, and capital does not apply to human ingenuity, which itself is a resource that goes into the production of our economic output. A better education system should increase the entrepreneurship of a nation's people, improving the nation's human capital.

D. Microeconomics and Macroeconomics

1. *Microeconomics* is the study of individual markets for goods, services, and resources.

   i. Microeconomics examines the supply and demand for a good or service in a particular market.

   ii. "Buyers" and "sellers" meet in markets to exchange money, goods, services, and resources. Equilibrium price and quantity occur when the quantity demanded for a particular item is equal to the quantity supplied.

   iii. Microeconomics examines the relationships between prices and quantities of individual products.

2. *Macroeconomics* is the study of whole nations' economies.

   i. Macroeconomics examines aggregates or the total sum of items examined individually in microeconomics, such as aggregate demand and aggregate supply, referring to the total demand for a nation's output and the total supply of the nation's output.

   ii. Macroeconomics examines the interactions of all of a nation's households, firms, government, and foreigners in determining the overall level of output, employment, and the price level in a nation.

   iii. Macroeconomics is used to inform government policy, which aims to achieve three main objectives:

   ➤ Full employment of the nation's labor force (low unemployment).

   ➤ Stability in the level of prices for goods and services in a nation (low inflation).

   ➤ The continual increase in the output of goods and services in a nation (economic growth).

II. Choice and Opportunity Cost

A. Choices are fundamental in economics, and scarcity necessitates choices.

1. Because the earth's resources are scarce (both desired and limited), choices must be made about how to allocate them between the competing wants and needs of society.

2. Individuals, firms, governments, and entire nations face trade-offs. A trade-off is the choice we face when deciding how to use our scarce resources.

3. Economic decisions require making informed choices by weighing the costs and benefits of the trade-offs we face.

B. All economic decisions involve costs.

1. Costs are those things that must be given up when we make a choice as to how to use our scarce resources.

2. "There is no such thing as a free lunch."

    i. Economists say "There is no such thing as a free lunch" because even when something appears to be "free" (in terms of its explicit cost or money price) there is always an implicit cost involved in undertaking any economic activity, even if that cost is as simple as what you could have done during the time it takes you to consume a so-called free lunch.

C. Opportunity cost is the opportunity lost.

1. The opportunity cost is what must be given up in order to undertake any activity or economic exchange.

2. Opportunity costs are not necessarily monetary; rather, when you buy something, the opportunity cost is what you could have done with the money you spent.

3. Even non-monetary exchanges involve opportunity costs, as you may have done something different with the time you chose to spend undertaking any activity in your life.

    i.   The opportunity cost of playing an hour of video games in the evening is the hour you could have spent studying.

    ii.   The opportunity cost of taking an AP Macroeconomics class is the knowledge you could have learned taking AP English instead.

    iii.   The opportunity cost of going to college is what you could have done with the money you spent on tuition, books, and room and board plus the income you could have earned getting a job after high school instead.

  4. All economic transactions involve opportunity costs.

III. Use of Models in Economics

A. What is a model?

  1. Models are tools used by scientists to represent objects, situations or scenarios from the real world.

  2. Economic models include diagrams and graphs that illustrate the relationships between two or more economic variables.

B. *Ceteris Paribus*

  1. *Ceteris paribus* is a Latin phrase that translates to "other things being equal."

  2. Economists assume *ceteris paribus* when using models to analyze the interactions between variables in the economy.

    i.   For example, one model used by economists is the aggregate demand diagram. This graph models the relationship between the price level of goods and services in a country and the quantity of all goods and services demanded by that nation's households, businesses, government, and foreigners.

    ii.   To analyze how the aggregate demand for a nation's output changes with the price level, economists assume that no other variables are changing, such as household income, the tax rate, foreign tastes and preferences, etc.

iii. While in the real world other variables are constantly changing, economists will often ignore this fact to focus on how one variable (aggregate demand) responds to a change in another variable (the price level of a nation's output).

IV. The Production Possibilities Curve or Frontier (PPC or PPF)

A. What the PPC Shows

1. The PPC is a simple economic model showing the trade-off an individual, business firm, government, or entire country faces in how to allocate scarce resources between two competing activities, goods, or services.

   i. The PPC models scarcity, since there is only a certain amount of any two goods that can be produced and consumed due to the limited nature of resources.

   ii. The PPC models efficiency, since when an individual, business, or nation produces or consumes inside its PPC, it is under-utilizing resources or using them inefficiently, whereas a point on the PPC represents full and productively efficient use of resources.

   iii. The PPC models opportunity cost, since it shows how much of one good must be given up in order to have additional units of another good.

B. An Individual's PPC

1. The PPC below shows the trade-off an individual faces between work and play during her 10 hours of free time over a weekend.

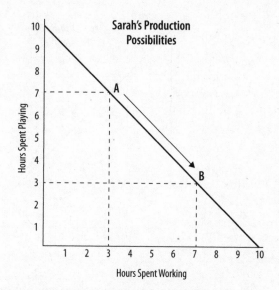

Sarah's Production Possibilities

i. Assume that point A represents Sarah's decision in week one, when she allocates seven hours to playing and three hours to working. Her decision to allocate her limited time in this manner involves an opportunity cost, which is the benefit she would have gained from spending more time working and less time playing.

ii. Assume that point B represents her decision in week two, when she has decided to spend seven hours working and only three playing. The opportunity cost of working four additional hours is the four fewer hours she gets to spend playing and all the enjoyment she forgoes as a result of her decision.

C. A Nation's PPC—Constant Opportunity Cost

1. A PPC may also represent the trade-offs faced by a nation in how to allocate its scarce resources between two possible goods or services. The PPC below shows Italy's choice of producing either pizzas or calzones.

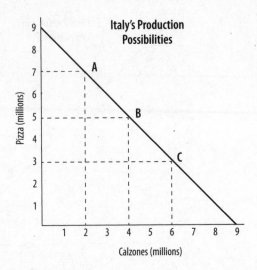

i. During any given production period, Italy can produce either nine million pizzas or nine million calzones, or any combination along the PPC, such as those indicated by points A, B, or C.

ii. The opportunity cost for one more calzone is always one pizza. The opportunity cost of pizzas and calzones is constant, since the two goods require similar types of labor, capital, and land resources to produce. Note that the opportunity cost is shown as the slope of the PPC. When the opportunity cost of producing a good does not change as more units of it are produced, the PPC is a straight line.

D. A Nation's PPC—Increasing Opportunity Cost

1. The two goods shown on a PPC will not always have a constant opportunity cost as society moves from the production of one to the other, as shown in the PPC below.

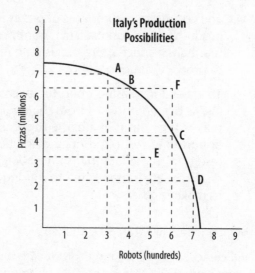

2. The Law of Increasing Opportunity Cost

   i. The PPC above has a convex shape, meaning it bows out from the origin.

   ii. Pizzas and robots require very different resources in their production. Pizzas are land intensive in production, since large amounts of land are needed to grow the ingredients. Pizzas also require a particular type of labor and capital; farmers and cooks need not have advanced degrees and extensive expertise in areas such as engineering to grow ingredients and make pizzas.

   iii. The land and labor resources required to make robots are very different than those for pizza. The type of labor needed to build robots is highly skilled and educated.

   iv. Because Italy's land, capital, and labor resources are not perfectly adaptable to making robots and pizzas, the opportunity cost of increasing production of robots increases in terms of pizzas the more robots are produced.

   v. Notice that the cost of the fourth robot Italy produces is just under one million pizzas, while the cost of the seventh robot is around two million pizzas.

vi. The cost of robots in terms of pizzas increases as Italy produces more robots. Each robot produced requires that Italy sacrifice more pizzas than it needed to give up to produce the prior robot.

vii. The law of increasing opportunity cost explains why the PPC is bowed outward from the origin. The law says that as the output of a particular product increases, the opportunity cost of producing additional units rises. This results from the fact that some labor, land, and capital resources are better suited to making some goods than to making others.

E. Other Concepts Illustrated by the PPC

1. Efficiency. When a nation is producing a combination of goods on its PPC (as in the case of points A, B, C, and D above), it is using its existing resources (land, labor and capital) efficiently.

   i. This means that nearly every person of working age who wants a job has a job, the land that can be used for production of pizza ingredients and robot components is being used, and the nation's existing capital (factory equipment, ovens, and other tools) is operating at its full capacity, meaning there is no capital sitting idle.

   ii. At points A, B, C, and D an increase in total output is not possible without an increase in inputs first. A nation achieving its production possibilities is producing at its full-employment level of output—it cannot increase production of either good without sacrificing output of the other.

2. Inefficiency. A nation not achieving full employment of resources is producing at a point inside its PPC. If Italy is producing 5 robots and 3.2 million pizzas (at point E above), it is under-utilizing its land, labor, and capital.

   i. A country is said to be inefficient if it is producing at a point inside of its PPC, meaning that unemployment is likely high, land that could be put into cultivation of food or production of minerals is not being used, and existing capital is sitting idle.

    ii.   An economy producing inside its PPC may be in a recession, meaning that the level of output has fallen below the full employment level achieved when producing on its PPC. Note that it would be possible to increase production of either good without giving anything up.

3. Economic Growth. A point beyond the nation's PPC is unattainable given the existing quantity and quality of resources, but clearly it is desirable since such a combination of output would mean more of everything. At point F in the model above, Italy could produce and consume six robots and over six million pizzas.

    i.   This point is clearly beyond Italy's current production possibilities, but it may be attainable in the future if Italy's economy grows.

    ii.   Economic growth is defined as an increase in the total output of a nation over time, which is possible if a nation experiences an increase in the quality or the quantity of productive resources.

    iii. In the future, Italy might be able to produce at a point like F if it experiences population growth, technological advancement, or an increase in capital stock.

4. Productivity. *Productivity* is defined as the output generated per unit of input.

    i.   If Italian workers become better at producing pizzas and robots, either through better training and education or through an increase in the quality of the technologies they possess to produce these goods, then the national output of Italy will grow and the country will move toward point F.

    ii.   Investments in public education by the government or investments in better technology and more capital by the country's businesses will lead to economic growth in Italy.

Expect a few questions in the multiple-choice section to involve production possibilities curves. The AP exam often asks about things such as what it means when a nation is producing inside its PPC, at a point on its PPC, and what would be necessary for a nation to produce beyond its current PPC. Questions about opportunity costs and trade-offs involving PPCs are also common.

V. Economic Systems

A. An *economic system* is the system a nation uses to allocate its scarce resource between the competing needs and wants of the nation's government, business firms, and households. There are two primary systems that have been used to allocate resources in the last century:

1. Command system

2. Market system

B. Three Basic Economic Questions. An economic system must address three basic economic questions, which arise because of the problem of scarcity.

1. What should be produced? Should society's scarce resources (land, labor and capital) be used to grow food, make clothes, toys, tools, weapons, or should they be used to provide services such as health care, entertainment, or haircuts?

2. How should it be produced? Should production be labor intensive or capital intensive? Should robots replace workers whenever possible, or should workers make up the majority of inputs into the production of goods and services? To what extent will technological innovation affect the way things are produced?

3. For whom should it be produced? Who will receive the output of the economy, and how much will each person receive? Should levels of consumption be based on social standing? Gender or age? Race or religion? Which goods and services should be regarded as needs and provided to

all, and which should only be enjoyed by those who can afford to pay the market price?

C. Command Economies

1. A *command economy* (often associated with communism or socialism) is an economic system in which the three basic economic questions are answered by the state.

2. All resources are allocated based on the priorities of the central government.

   i.   If equality is the goal, then the nation's resources and the output they produce will be distributed evenly among households.

   ii. If military strength is the goal, then more resources will go toward the production of weapons than toward consumer products.

3. No private ownership or property rights. In a command economy, the state owns all factors of production. The lack of private ownership of resources often creates a problem of incentives.

   i.   When the only goal of producers is to meet the quotas sent down by the state, resources are often wasted or used inefficiently.

   ii. Command economies have mostly transitioned to a market system because of the enormous inefficiency in the allocation and use of resources resulting from the lack of private ownership and incentives.

D. Market Economies

1. Market economies are based on the principles of private ownership of resources, property rights, and the pursuit of self-interest. Resources tend to flow toward the most profitable uses, and goods are allocated to those willing and able to pay the most for them.

2. Adam Smith was the eighteenth-century Scottish social philosopher whose observations of European society, captured in his book *The Wealth of Nations*, form the basis for market (or *laissez-faire*) economic theory.

3. Smith observed: *"It is not from the benevolence of the butcher, the brewer, or the baker that we expect our dinner, but from their regard to their own self-interest. We address ourselves, not to their humanity but to their self-love, and never talk to them of our own necessities but of their advantages."*

4. In a market economy, resources are allocated and used relatively efficiently because it is in the self-interest of individuals to meet the needs of society, thereby earning for themselves an income that they can then use to meet their own wants and needs.

5. Market economies function based on three fundamental characteristics:

   i. Property Rights. When individuals have ownership of their private resources (land, labor, capital) and this ownership is protected by law, they are free to employ their resources toward whatever activity they chose.

   ii. Incentives. The incentive of individuals in a market economy is to maximize their utility (economic term meaning happiness). The incentive of each firm is to maximize its profit. In their pursuit of economic profits, firms will produce the goods and services that bring the greatest utility to households. The market thereby provides greater total welfare to society than a command economy controlled by a central government could hope to achieve.

   iii. Prices. The price mechanism allows buyers in a market to send signals to producers of how much of particular goods or services are demanded. Prices reflect the relative demand and supply of different goods. If something is in great demand or limited supply, its price tends to rise, creating the incentive for businesses to produce more of it and consumers to demand less of it. Prices regulate the allocation and use of resources in a market economy.

E. The Circular Flow in a Market Economy

   1. Fundamental to the market economic system is the idea that the exchanges between individuals are voluntary and that anyone engaging in such exchanges benefits.

2. This implies that when one person voluntarily gives another something that the second person wants, the first person must be getting something he wants in return. Thus both parties are better off following the exchange.

3. All exchanges in a market economy take place in either the product market or the resource market. The demand for resources by business firms and for goods and services by households is met in one of these two markets.

   i.   Households are the owners of productive resources, which are the inputs firms need in order to produce goods and services.

   ii. To acquire the inputs for production, firms must pay households for their resources in the resource market.

   iii. Households earn their income in the resource market and then demand the finished products provided by firms in the product market.

   iv. The flow of resources, money, and goods and services is illustrated in a model economists call the circular flow model.

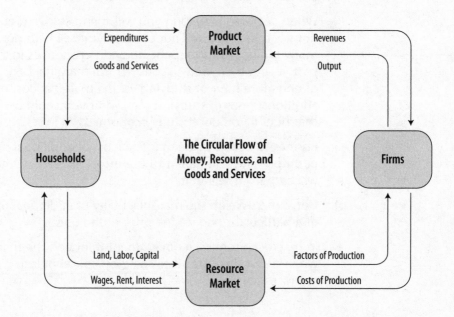

4. The circular flow diagram above is a simple model and does not account for the role of government or foreign consumers in a nation's economy. In a later chapter we will revisit the circular flow including these two important stakeholders.

The circular flow model is not one you will commonly see or be asked to draw on the AP exam. So why know it? Understanding the concepts illustrated in this model, specifically the interdependence of households and firms in a market economy and the exchanges that take place in product and resource markets, is foundational to your knowledge of the other topics that will be tested on the exam.

VI. Marginal Analysis

A. Economic decisions take place on the margin.

1. *Marginal* is defined as "additional" or "change in."

2. An economic decision by an individual, a business firm, or a government is usually a marginal decision. For example:

   i. When deciding how long you will spend studying economics today, you will not concern yourself with how many hours you have spent studying economics in the past year, rather you will consider the marginal benefit of one more hour of studying vs. the marginal cost of an additional hour of studying (i.e., what you could do in that hour if you don't study economics).

   ii. Businesses consider the marginal cost of additional units of output and compare it to the marginal revenue they will earn from selling it.

   iii. Consumers weigh the marginal utility of additional units of a particular good vs. the price of the good.

   iv. In macroeconomics, a government thinks on the margin when determining tax rates paid by households at different income levels

v. When determining fiscal policy, a government must consider the marginal propensity to consume and the marginal propensity to save of its nation's households. This will help the government determine the relative effect of either a change in taxes or a change in government spending.

3. Marginal anything refers to the change in the total.

VII. Comparative Advantage, Absolute Advantage, Specialization, and Trade

A. When an individual or a nation specializes in the production of a particular good or service and trades for all other goods or services, the total output and welfare of society is increased.

B. Absolute Advantage

1. A country or individual has an absolute advantage in the production of a good when it can produce it using fewer resources than another country or individual. For example:

    i. If the United States can produce 13 million cell phones using 1,000 workers and Korea can produce only 12 million cell phones using 1,000 workers, then the United States has an absolute advantage in the production of cell phones.

    ii. If the United States can grow 39 million apples using 1,000 workers and Korea can grow only 24 million apples using the same amount of labor, then the United States has an absolute advantage in apples.

2. Absolute Advantage in a Production Possibilities Table

Country/Good	Cell Phones Produced by 1,000 Workers (millions)	Apples Grown by 1,000 Workers (millions)
United States	13	39
Korea	12	24

    i.   The table above shows the production possibilities for two nations of cell phones and apples.

    ii. The United States has an absolute advantage in both goods since it can produce more apples and more cell phones using 1,000 workers.

C. Comparative Advantage

  1. A country has a comparative advantage in production of a certain product when it can produce that product at a lower relative opportunity cost than another country.

    i.   To determine which country has a comparative advantage in apples, you must calculate the opportunity cost of apples in the United States and in Korea.

    ii. To grow 39 million apples, the United States must give up 13 million cell phones. Therefore each apple "costs" the United States $\frac{13}{39}$ = 0.33 cell phones.

    iii. To grow 24 million apples in Korea, 12 million cell phones must be given up. Each apple "costs" Korea $\frac{12}{24}$ = 0.5 cell phones.

    iv. The opportunity cost of an apple in the United States is only 0.33 cell phones, while the opportunity cost of an apple in Korea is 0.5 cell phones.

    v. The United States has a comparative advantage in the production of apples, because it costs the United States fewer cell phones in order to make an apple than it costs Korea.

  2. To determine which country has a comparative advantage in cell phones, you must calculate the opportunity cost of cell phones in the United States and Korea.

    i.   To produce 13 million cell phones, the United States gives up 39 million apples. Each cell phone costs $\frac{39}{13}$ = 3 apples.

ii. To produce 12 million cell phones, Korea gives up 24 million apples, so each cell phone costs Korea $\frac{24}{12}$ = 2 apples.

iii. The opportunity cost of cell phones is lower in Korea than the United States.

iv. Korea has a comparative advantage in the production of cell phones, because it costs Korea fewer apples to make a cell phone than it costs the United States.

3. Note that a country could never have a comparative advantage in production of both goods, because the opportunity cost of one good is the reciprocal of the other good.

D. Specialization and trade should be based on comparative advantage, not absolute advantage.

1. Countries should specialize in the production of the good or goods for which they have a comparative advantage over other countries, and trade for other goods. Such trading allows each country to reduce its opportunity cost of the good it imports.

i. In our example, Korea should specialize in cell phones, the United States in apples, and the two countries should trade with one another.

ii. Both countries can benefit from trade by taking advantage of the other country's lower opportunity cost for the good in which it specializes. For example:

➤ Assume the two countries specialize and trade with one another at a rate of 2.5 apples per cell phone, or 0.4 cell phones per apple.

➤ The United States gains from trade because domestically, each cell phone would have cost three apples, but with trade the United States only gives up two and one-half apples per cell phone.

➤ Korea gains from trade because domestically, each apple would have cost 0.5 cell phones, but with trade it only gives up 0.4 cell phones $\left(\dfrac{1}{2.5}\right)$ per apple.

E. A PPC can be used to show how gains from trade allow countries to enjoy combinations of good that they could not produce domestically.

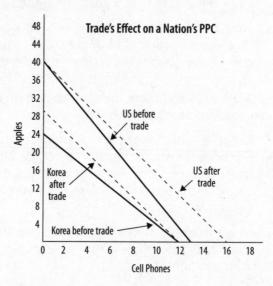

1. In the graph above, the information from the production possibilities table for Korea and the United States has been graphed in a PPC. Without trade, each nation can consume only a combination of apples and cell phones along their domestic PPCs.

2. With trade, the nations specialize in the good for which they have the lower opportunity cost (the Unites States in apples, Korea in cell phones). They then trade with one another for the other good at a rate that is better than what they would have faced by producing the other good domestically.

3. The dotted lines represent the nations' trading possibilities curves. Notice that the total amount of apples and cell

phones able to be consumed by the United States and Korea is greater with trade than without.

F. Specialization and trade based on the principle of comparative advantage increases the productivity of a nation's resources and allows for greater total output than would otherwise be possible.

The basic economic concepts found in this chapter are tested on both the AP Micro and Macro exams. If you're taking the two courses together, don't forget to study this unit in preparation for both exams. It would not be unusual for some of the same (or at least very similar) questions to show up on both exams in a year. You can expect around six questions on these basic economic concepts in the multiple-choice section.

Supply, Demand, and Equilibrium
in Product Markets

 I. **Demand and Its Determinants**

A. *Demand* is a schedule or a curve representing the willingness and ability of all the buyers in a market to buy a particular good at a range of prices during a particular period of time.

B. The demand for a particular good is a microeconomic concept, since it relates quantity demanded of a particular good or service to its price, as opposed to an entire nation's output of goods and services.

C. Demand for a good is inversely related to the price of the good.

1. At higher prices, consumers generally demand a lower quantity of a good.

2. At lower prices, greater quantities are demanded.

D. The law of demand states that there is an inverse relationship between the price of a good and the quantity demanded.

1. The law of demand can be illustrated in a Demand Curve diagram.

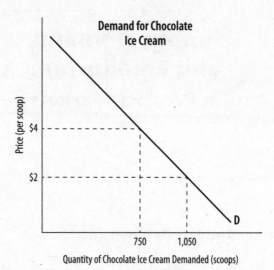

Demand for Chocolate Ice Cream

Price (per scoop)

$4

$2

750   1,050

D

Quantity of Chocolate Ice Cream Demanded (scoops)

2. In the market for chocolate ice cream, the demand is illustrated as a downward sloping line, inversely related to the price of ice cream.

3. At $4 per scoop, consumers in this market will demand only 750 scoops of chocolate ice cream. But when the price decreases to $2 per scoop, the quantity demanded increases to 1,000 scoops.

4. At lower prices, more consumers wish to buy chocolate ice cream and those already buying ice cream wish to purchase more scoops.

E. Changes in quantity demanded are distinct from changes in demand.

1. A change in the price of chocolate ice cream (or any good) leads to a movement along the demand curve and a change in the quantity of the good demanded.

2. Anything that changes the demand for ice cream (or any good) will cause the entire demand curve to shift.

i. If demand increases, it shifts to the right and a greater quantity is demanded at each of the series of prices shown on the demand diagram.

ii. If demand decreases, it shifts to the left and a lesser quantity is demanded at each of the prices shown on the diagram.

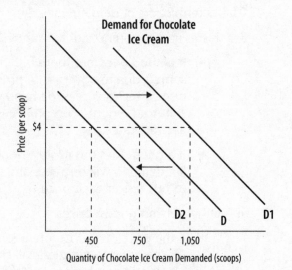

Demand for Chocolate Ice Cream

Quantity of Chocolate Ice Cream Demanded (scoops)

iii. In the graph above, a shift in demand from D to D1 represents an increase in demand. At $4 per scoop, 1,050 scoops would now be demanded by consumers.

iv. A shift in demand from D to D2 represents a decrease in demand. At $4, consumers now wish to buy only 450 scoops of ice cream.

3. There is a clear difference between a change in quantity demanded for a good and a change in demand for a good. If only price changes, quantity changes (shown as a movement along a fixed demand curve), but if one of the determinants of demand changes, the entire demand curve will shift.

F. The Determinants of Demand

1. The demand for any particular good is determined by the price of the good, but also several non-price determinants of demand.

2. A change in any of the non-price determinants of demand will shift a demand curve inward (if demand decreases) or outward (if demand increases).

3. The determinants of demand include:

   i.   Tastes and preferences of consumers.

     ➤ If a good becomes more fashionable among consumers due to advertising, product improvement, or new technologies, demand will increase and shift to the right. Consumers will wish to buy more at every price.

     ➤ If a good goes out of style or becomes less popular, demand will decrease and consumers will wish to buy less at each price.

   ii.   Other related goods' prices.

     ➤ If the price of a substitute good changes, demand for the good in question will change. Assume pizzas and hamburgers are substitutes for one another (both are fast-food items that you can choose between for dinner). If pizza becomes more expensive, consumers will demand more of its substitute, hamburgers.

     ➤ If the price of a complementary good changes, demand changes. Complementary goods are things that are consumed together, like hamburgers and hamburger buns. If hamburgers get more expensive, fewer people will eat them, so demand for buns decreases.

   iii. Consumer expectations.

     ➤ If consumers expect their incomes to rise in the future, they are likely to demand more of most goods now.

     ➤ If consumers expect the price of a good to change, it may also affect their demand now. The expectation of higher prices in the future will increase demand for most goods in the present.

iv. Consumers' incomes.

➤ For normal goods, as consumers' incomes rise, the demand increases.

➤ For inferior goods (such as discount toilet paper), an increase in consumers' incomes leads to a fall in demand, as consumers substitute higher-quality, normal goods instead.

v. The number of consumers. Naturally, if more consumers enter a market, the demand for the good in the market will increase. If the number of consumers decreases, demand will decrease.

4. A change in any of these factors will shift the demand for a good, changing the quantity consumers wish to buy at each of the prices, and appearing as a shift of the entire demand curve as shown above.

Test Tip

A typical question about the determinants of demand will go something like this: **Which of the following will cause the demand for _____ to increase/decrease?** *Based on your knowledge of the good in question, you must choose from the five possible answer choices the one that is most likely a determinant of demand.*

II. Supply and Its Determinants

A. *Supply* is a schedule or a curve showing the various quantities of a particular good firms are willing and able to produce at a series of prices in a given period of time.

B. Like demand, supply is a microeconomic concept, since it refers to the supply for a particular good, rather than the total supply for all a nation's goods and services.

C. Supply of a good is directly related to the price of that good.

1. At higher prices, more firms find it profitable to produce a good; therefore, the quantity supplied increases as the price increases.

2. At lower prices, firms find it harder to cover their costs of production, so fewer firms will be willing and able to produce the good.

D. The law of supply states that there is a direct relationship between the price of a good and the quantity supplied by firms.

1. The law of supply can be illustrated in a Supply Curve.

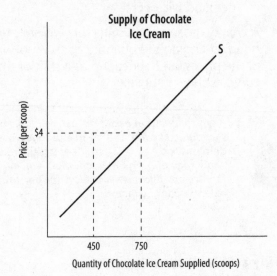

Quantity of Chocolate Ice Cream Supplied (scoops)

2. In the market for chocolate ice cream, the supply is illustrated as an upward sloping line, showing a direct relationship between the price per scoop and the number of scoops supplied.

3. At a low price of $2 per scoop, fewer sellers will find it profitable to produce chocolate ice cream, so only 450 scoops will be produced. But when the price per scoop rises to $4, more ice cream makers will wish to produce chocolate ice cream and the quantity supplied increases to 750 scoops.

4. At higher prices, more producers wish to produce chocolate ice cream.

E. Changes in Quantity Supplied vs. Changes in Supply.

1. Just like demand, a change in the price of a good leads to a movement along the supply curve and a change in the quantity supplied.

2. Anything that changes the supply of a good would cause the entire supply curve to shift:

    i.   to the left (if supply decreases) or

    ii. to the right (if supply increases).

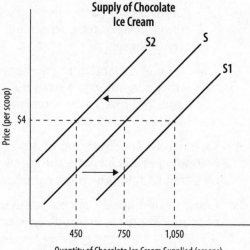

Quantity of Chocolate Ice Cream Supplied (scoops)

 iii. In the graph above, a shift from S to S1 represents an increase in supply. At $4, producers would now be willing to produce 1,050 scoops of chocolate ice cream.

 iv. A shift from S to S2 represents a decrease in supply. Producers are now willing to produce only 450 scoops of ice cream.

3. There is a difference between a change in quantity supplied (which results from a change in the price) and a change in supply (which is the result of a change in one of the determinants of supply).

F. The Determinants of Supply

1. The supply of any particular good is determined by the price of the good, but also by several non-price determinants.

2. A change in any of the non-price determinants of supply causes the supply curve to shift left or right, signifying either a decrease or an increase in supply, respectively.

3. The determinants of supply include:

   i. Subsidies and taxes.

      ➤ A subsidy is a payment from the government to a producer for each unit produced. A subsidy lowers firms' costs of production and results in an increase in supply.

      ➤ A tax is a mandatory payment from producers to the government for each unit produced. A tax adds to firms' costs of production and results in a decrease in supply.

   ii. Technology. The invention of productivity-enhancing technologies will increase the supply of goods that employ that technology in their production.

   iii. Other related goods' prices. Some producers are capable of producing more than one type of good with their resources.

      ➤ Substitutes in Production. If a related good made from similar input goes up in price, producers may switch their production to those goods, increasing their supply and reducing the supply of the primary good. For example, if the price of plastic pens rises, then the manufacturer may decide to allocate more of its plastic to pen making and the supply of disposable razors may shift to the left.

      ➤ Complements in Production. If two goods are produced together, then an increase in the price of one leads to an increase in the supply of the other. For example, if the price of beef rises, ranchers will increase the quantity of beef produced and as a result the supply of leather may shift to the right.

iv. Resource costs. If the costs of the resources firms use in production decrease, supply of the output increases. When costs rise, supply decreases.

v.   Producers' expectations. If producers expect the price of their output to rise in the future, or they expect the incomes of their consumers to increase, they will increase their supply of those goods. If they expect future demand to be low, they will reduce supply.

vi. The number of firms in a market. If new firms enter a market and begin producing a good, the market supply of that good increases. If firms leave the market, supply decreases.

4. A change in any of the determinants of supply will cause supply to either increase and shift to the right or decrease and shift to the left.

Test Tip

Although supply and demand is a micro concept, questions on these concepts occasionally appear on the macro exam. Since a nation's economy is made up of individual markets, understanding how supply and demand interact in markets is fundamental to understanding how a national economy functions.

III. Market Equilibrium

A. The equilibrium price and quantity of any good is determined by the supply and demand for that good in the marketplace.

B. The price at which the quantity demanded by consumers equals the quantity supplied by firms is known as the equilibrium price. The quantity is known as the equilibrium quantity.

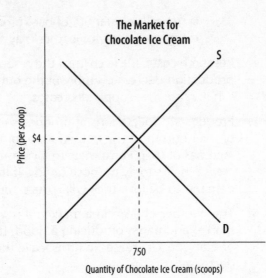

The Market for Chocolate Ice Cream

Price (per scoop)

$4

750

Quantity of Chocolate Ice Cream (scoops)

1. In the graph above, at a price of $4 both the quantity supplied and the quantity demanded is 750 scoops.

2. The market is in equilibrium, because there are no consumers who wish they could have ice cream nor are there producers who wish they could sell their ice cream. The equilibrium is the unique price-quantity combination at which the market clears, in other words, at which the quantity supplied is exactly equal to the quantity demanded and neither a shortage nor surplus exists.

C. A change in either demand or supply will result in a new equilibrium price and quantity.

1. If any of the determinants of demand change, demand will either increase or decrease.

    i. An increase in demand (from D to D1) causes the equilibrium price and quantity to rise.

    ii. A decrease in demand (from D to D2) causes the equilibrium price and quantity to decrease.

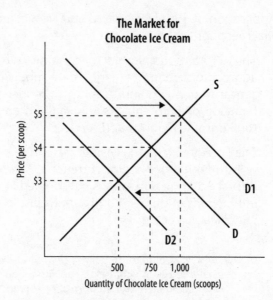

2. If any of the determinants of supply change, supply will either increase or decrease.

    i.   An increase in supply (from S to S1) causes the equilibrium price to decrease and the quantity to increase.

    ii. A decrease in supply (from S to S2) causes the equilibrium price to increase and the quantity to decrease.

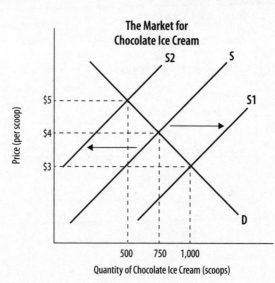

D. Application of Supply, Demand and Market Equilibrium to Macroeconomics

1. The AD/AS model. In macroeconomics, you will study the aggregate demand and aggregate supply model. While similar to demand and supply, this model examines the interaction of all the buyers and all the producers of a nation's total output of goods and services.

2. The Foreign Exchange Market. Also in macroeconomics you will study the markets for currencies. The price of a currency is the exchange rate, and is determined in a market by the interactions of demand and supply, just like the price of chocolate ice cream.

Sometimes a question doesn't ask about demand or supply itself, but about changes in equilibrium price or quantity, and what could have caused particular changes. Such a question would require you to synthesize your knowledge of the determinants of both demand and supply and apply that knowledge to find the effect of shifts in both curves. For example: **Which of the following shifts in supply and demand would definitely cause the equilibrium price to decrease and the quantity to increase?** *In such a question, it may help to sketch graphs on some scratch paper, which would help you conclude that an increase in supply and no change in demand would result in the described outcome.*

PART III

MEASUREMENT OF ECONOMIC PERFORMANCE

National Income Accounts

 The Circular Flow of the Macroeconomy

A. Significance of the Circular Flow

1. A modern market economy includes several stakeholders who interact in the marketplace supplying and demanding goods, services, and productive resources.

2. The interactions of the various stakeholders can be represented in a model showing the flow of money that facilitates exchanges in product and resource markets.

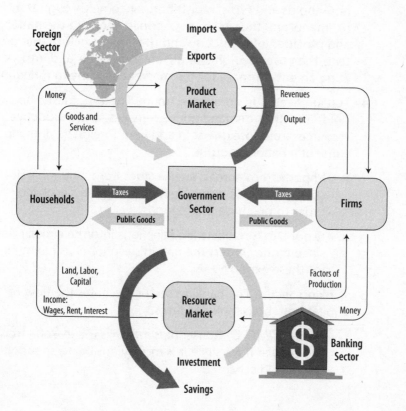

B. The five contributors to the economic activity in a nation's economy include:

1. Households. Domestic households demand goods and services in the product market; supply land, labor, and capital in the resource market; pay taxes to the government, receive transfer payments and the provision of public goods from the government; and demand imports from foreign countries.

2. Firms. Domestic business firms produce many of the goods and services consumed by households. Firms demand productive resources (land, labor, and capital) from households in the resource market. Firms pay taxes to the government and enjoy public goods and services provided by the government. Some firms sell their output to foreign consumers and demand resources from foreign households.

3. Government Sector. The macroeconomic circular flow model includes the government, which collects taxes from households and firms, redistributes income through transfer payments and the provision of public goods to the nation, and provides infrastructure and the legal structure that protects the property rights of private individuals and firms, creating an environment for the market economy to function.

4. Foreign Sector. In an open economy, both domestic households and firms demand goods, services, and productive resources from foreigners. In addition, foreigners demand some of a nation's output.

   i. Imports from abroad are leakages from a nation's circular flow, since money leaves the nation's economy in order to purchase these goods.

   ii. Exports to foreigners are injections into the circular flow, since money enters the nation's economy as payment for these exports.

5. Banking Sector. The banking sector facilitates the flow of capital from households to firms.

   i. Money saved by households in banks is a leakage from the circular flow, since it is money not being spent on goods and services.

    ii. Money lent to firms or households for investment is an injection into the circular flow, since firms are spending on new capital, leading to more employment and output.

    iii. A bank functions as a convenient intermediary, allowing lenders and borrowers to do business finding one another.

C. Two market types are featured in the circular flow. The circular flow of a nation's economy is based on the exchanges that take place in two markets where buyers and sellers meet.

  1. Resource Market. These are the markets in which business firms acquire productive resources from households. Resource markets include:

    i. Labor Markets. Households provide labor to firms. In exchange for their labor, households receive money payments from firms in the form of wages. If a business owner is self-employed, the opportunity cost of working for himself or herself is the wages he or she could have earned working for someone else.

    ii. Capital Markets. Households who save provide financial capital to banks, which make loans to firms wishing to acquire new physical capital. In exchange for their physical capital, households receive money payments in the form of interest. If a business owner uses his or her own finances to acquire capital for his or her business, the opportunity cost of spending money on capital is the interest that could have been earned saving the money in a bank.

    iii. Land Markets. Firms may need to rent the space in which they operate their business. Households that own the land, retail, warehouse, or factory space receive rent from firms in exchange for its use. If the business owner uses his or her own land in production, the opportunity cost of using the self-owned resources is the rent he or she could have earned by renting the land out to another business.

     iv. Though markets for entrepreneurial ability are often not as formal, profit serves as a cue to entrepreneurs, pulling them toward better business opportunities. Because the innovative talents for combining the other three resources are owned by the entrepreneur, the opportunity cost of using these self-owned talents is known as normal profit, or the amount that the business owner could have earned putting those talents to use doing something else (running a different business or working for someone else).

  2. **Product Market.** This represents the markets in which households demand the goods and services produced by firms.

     i. *Goods* refers to any physical products such as food, clothes, cars, and televisions.

     ii. *Services* refers to non-tangible products such as legal and financial services, haircuts, taxi rides, tourism, and education.

D. **Injections and Leakages from a Nation's Circular Flow.** The flow of money in a nation experiences constant injections and leakages.

  1. Injections create more spending, production, and employment in an economy and thus increase the overall size of the nation's economy.

  2. Leakages reduce the amount of spending, production, and employment in a nation, and thus reduce the overall size of the nation's economy.

  3. The Government Sector

     i. Leakages. Taxes paid by households and firms on income, revenues, profits, and consumption reduce the flow of income in the economy. Money paid to the government is money households or firms cannot spend on goods, services, or investments in capital and labor.

     ii. Injections. Government provides goods and services to the nation's households and firms as well as transferring payments that redistributes the nation's income. Goods and services provided by government include education, infrastructure, the legal and judicial system, public safety, national defense, and others. Transfer payments include government programs that transfer the nation's income from certain taxpayers to other stakeholders such as welfare, unemployment, Social Security, subsidies to certain producers, and financial aid for education.

   iii. When government pulls more money out of the circular flow in taxes than it injects through spending, it is acting to slow the economy down and running a budget surplus. If government spends more than it taxes, it is acting to stimulate the economy and running a budget deficit.

4. The Banking Sector

   i. Leakages. Money saved in banks by households and firms is considered a leakage from the circular flow, because money saved is money not spent on output, not going toward creating employment.

   ii. Injections. Money borrowed from banks by households and firms to finance spending on consumer goods and capital goods is an injection into the circular flow, because such spending leads to more employment, increasing the nation's output and the income of households.

5. The Foreign Sector

   i. Leakages. Import spending by domestic households on foreign-produced goods and services is leakage from the nation's circular flow because that money is *not* being spent on domestic output and is *not* going to contribute to domestic employment.

   ii. Injections. Export revenues from the sale of goods and services to foreign households and firms is an injection into the nation's circular flow because it creates greater demand for the nation's output, increasing employment and income among domestic households.

II. Gross Domestic Product and Its Components

A. The circular flow model illustrates the idea that all the spending in the economy will roughly equal all of the income received.

1. Every dollar spent on a good, service, or resource is a dollar earned by a household or a firm. Therefore, the nation's expenditures equal the nation's income.

2. Since everything bought was at some point produced, the nation's income is equal to the nation's output.

3. Economists use three methods for measuring a nation's total output:

    i. Expenditure approach;

    ii. Income approach;

    iii. Output approach.

4. Each of these approaches seeks to ascertain the value of output or income in a given year, in the hopes of quantifying the level of activity in the economy. Each approach seeks to measure the country's gross domestic product (GDP), which is the total market value of all the goods and services produced within a country during a year.

B. The Expenditure Approach to Measuring GDP

1. Counts the total spending on final new goods and services in a given year.

    i. "Final" goods are ready for consumption and do not include goods that will be input goods or are raw materials for other production.

    ➤ Apples bought at the grocery store count.

    ➤ Apples sold to a baker for apple pie are not counted until the pie is sold in its final form.

2. This approach distinguishes between four types of spending on a nation's output:

    i. Consumption (C). Consumption measures all spending by domestic households on durable and non-durable goods and services during a particular period of time. Consumption is a function of households' disposable income and their marginal propensity to consume (MPC).

➤ Durable Goods. These are generally defined as goods that last more than one year. Large appliances, such as refrigerators, televisions, and automobiles, are considered durable goods.

➤ Non-durable Goods. Goods that do not last as long as a year are considered non-durable goods. Rapidly consumed goods like food, magazines, health and beauty products, soaps and detergents are all examples of non-durable goods.

➤ Services. Services are actions performed by a firm. Legal services, insurance, sales firms, health care, and education are all examples of services counted in GDP statistics.

ii. Investment (I). *Investment* is short for "gross domestic private investment," and measures the total spending by firms on capital equipment and by households on newly constructed homes. The level of investment in a nation is a function of the national output and the interest rate.

iii. Government Spending (G). *Government spending* is short for gross "government investment and spending" and measures a country's government's expenditures on goods and services, including salaries for government workers as well as capital goods spending. Not included are transfer payments. Transfer payments (tax revenue redistributed to pensioners, veterans, and the unemployed) do not represent any new production and are thus excluded.

iv. Net Exports (Xn or X – M): Net exports measures the total income earned from the sale of exports (X) to foreign households, firms, and governments minus the total amount spent by domestic households, firms, and government on goods and services imported (M) from other nations. Net exports can be negative or positive, depending on whether a nation spends more on imports than it earns from the sale of its exports. For example, in the United States, which imports far more than it exports, net exports are negative. This is called a trade deficit. China, which exports more than it imports, has a trade surplus, hence a positive net exports.

3. Taken together, the expenditure approach can be expressed as $GDP = C + I + G + Xn$.

4. An example of the expenditure method is shown below. This shows the spending totals for each sector in the United States economy for 2009.

Expenditure Category	Billions of USD
Personal consumption expenditure (C)	$10,001
Gross private domestic investment (I)	$1,589
Government expenditures (G)	$2,914
Net export goods and services (X)	–$386
Gross domestic product	$14,118

C. The Income Approach to Measuring GDP

1. Measures GDP by recording the income of households in the resource market side of the circular flow of income.

2. If all spending on goods and services creates revenue to the firms providing the products, and the revenue earned by firms goes toward paying households for the land, labor, capital, and entrepreneurship employed in production, then it must be possible to arrive at an accurate measure of GDP by counting the income received by households in a given year.

3. Explains why "national output" is sometimes referred to as "national income." Output equals income in a nation.

4. National income includes payments households receive in the resource market in exchange for providing firms with the factors of production, including the total sum of each of the following earned by a nation's households in a year:

   i.   Wages. This is the payment households receive for providing their labor in the resource market. Wages (and salaries) usually make up the largest component of GDP in a nation.

   ii. Interest. Interest is the payment for the use of capital by firms. Much capital spending is paid for with money borrowed from banks. The money in banks is mostly households' savings. In exchange for the use of households' money, firms pay interest and thereby acquire new capital equipment.

   iii. Rent. Rent is the payment households receive in exchange for the use of their land. Businesses will pay rent to use factory or office space, and those firms that employ land owned by the firm forgo the opportunity cost of renting their land out to other businesses.

   iv. Profits. Profits are the payments entrepreneurs seek for their own endeavors in the resource market. Business owners seek profits when starting a new business.

Income Category	Billions USD
Compensation of employees (W)	$7,819.5
Interest payments (I)	$2,843.6
Rental incomes (R)	$274
Profits (P)	$2,957.3
Statistical discrepancy	$224.6
Gross domestic product	$14,119

5. Net national income is the income earned by households as payments for providing the four factors of production, minus taxes and the depreciation of capital.

6. To arrive at GDP, each of the following is added to the net national income:

    i. Business Taxes. These are taxes paid for goods that were actually produced, thus must be added to income to arrive at total national income.

    ii. Fixed Capital Consumption. This is another term for depreciation, an accounting term that reflects the drop in value for assets as they become used or worn. Capital is consumed and therefore some spending goes to the replacement of that capital.

    iii. Net Foreign Factor Income. This measures the difference between factor payments (wages, interest, rent, and profit) received from the foreign sector by domestic households and factor payments made to foreign citizens for domestic production.

    iv. Statistical Discrepancy. This measure resolves the fact that the income method is not as exact in calculating GDP as that of the expenditure method.

7. By adding up all the income earned in a nation in a given year, we arrive at a GDP figure that corresponds with the same figure found by adding up all the expenditures made on a nation's output in a year. United States GDP in 2009 equaled $14,119 billion, whether we used the expenditure approach or the income approach.

D. The Output Approach

1. Like the other methods for measuring GDP, the output approach measures the total value of all final goods and services produced by a country in a year.

2. The output approach measures the value of the total output produced in different sectors of the economy. When the total output of each sector of the nation's economy is summed, total output is found.

Output Category	Billions USD
Agriculture, forestry, fishing, hunting	$99.6
Mining	$196.1
Utilities	$184.3
Construction	$518.6
Manufacturing	$1,215.2
Transportation, warehousing	$337.9
Wholesale trade	$706.1
Retail trade	$812.4
Information	$423.2
Professional and business services	$1,684.8
Educational, health care, social assistance	$1,244.8
Arts, entertainment, recreation, accommodation, food services	$453
Other services	$352
Government	$1,897.2
Rest of world	$146.3
National income	$12,173
Capital consumption	$1,861
Statistical adjustment	$85
Gross domestic product	$14,119

3. The sum of all the value of the output of each sector of the United States economy gives us the gross domestic product.

4. The three methods all achieve the same result:
   GDP = National expenditures = National income = National output.

III. Real vs. Nominal Gross Domestic Product

A. Nominal GDP measures the value of a nation's output produced in a year, expressed in the value of the prices charged for that year. But if the average price level of a nation's output increases in a year, the nominal GDP could increase even if the actual amount of output does not change. It might appear that GDP had increased by quite a lot when in fact the same number of goods and services had been produced.

1. For example, a car is manufactured and sold for $20,000 in a given year. One year later, the same car is manufactured and sold for $25,000.

2. Simple math tells us that the price has increased by 25 percent, but nothing about the car is actually 25 percent greater than in the previous year.

3. So a nominal measure of GDP for the second year would count this 25 percent increase in price as a contribution to national income, when really it is only an increase in the price of the good.

4. It is in this way that price increases from inflation could cause GDP to be overestimated, causing us to think the economy is doing better than it is in reality.

B. Measuring Real GDP—The Use of Price Indexes

1. To determine the change in the real GDP (the actual output of a nation adjusted for changes in the price level), economists must adjust the nominal value of the nation's output in a year based on any changes in the average price level of goods and services during that year.

   i. In the case of the price level increasing (inflation): nominal GDP exaggerates value of output compared to real output.

   ii. In the case of the price level decreasing (deflation): nominal GDP underestimates value of real output compared to actual output.

2. To determine whether nominal GDP over or understates the real output of the nation, it first must be determined wheth-

er the average price level increased or decreased. To do this, economists use a price index known as the GDP deflator.

i. A price index measures the change in the price of a particular basket of goods between one period of time and another.

ii. The goods included in a nation's GDP deflator are determined by the government agency responsible for calculating it. In the United States this agency is the Bureau of Economic Analysis.

3. The GDP deflator is found by taking the total price of a particular basket of goods in one month and dividing it by the total price of the same basket of goods in another month, and multiplying the result by 100.

$$\text{GDP Deflator} = \frac{\text{Price of selected goods in current year}}{\text{Price of selected goods in base year}} \times 100$$

i. It is called a deflator because in most cases a nation's nominal GDP will be overstated from one year to the next due to a rise in the price level, or inflation.

ii. Normally, this index will deflate nominal GDP to a smaller number that reflects the actual output in one year based on the value of the dollar in a base year.

iii. This price-adjusted number is called real GDP, because it factors out inflation and deflation, and better reflects the true measure of goods and services produced that year.

4. The GDP deflator will always be expressed as a number indexed to a base year. The index for the base year itself is 100.

i. In years in which the price of the basket of goods is higher, the index will be greater than 100.

ii. When the price level in a year is below that of the base year, the index will be below 100.

5. The table below shows the United States nominal GDP and the GDP deflator with a base year of 2005 from 2005 to 2009[1].

---

[1] Source: *http://bea.gov/*

Year	Nominal GDP	GDP Deflator	Real GDP
2005	12,638.4	100	12,638.4
2006	13,398.9	103.25	12,976.2
2007	14,061.8	106.29	13,228.9
2008	14,369.1	108.61	13,228.8
2009	14,119.0	109.61	12,880.6

i.   The base year is 2005. Changes in price for all goods and services are measured against the price of the basket established in 2005. When the basket prices are compiled again, the final numbers are expressed as a change in percentage compared to the base year.

ii.   For example, in 2005 the index is established at 100. In 2006, the price of the same basket of goods was 3.25 percent higher than in 2005, so the GDP deflator is

$$103.25 = \left(\frac{103.25}{100}\right) \times 100 .$$

iii.   In 2007, prices increased further compared to the base year, and the GDP deflator has increased to 106.29, indicating that prices were 6.29 percent higher than in 2005.

iv.   The United States experienced an increase in the price of the goods measured for the GDP deflator every year between 2005 and 2009, increasing a total of 9.61 percent over the period.

6. With the GDP deflator established, it is possible to convert the nominal value of the nation's output in all five years into a real GDP by adjusting the nominal figure for changes in the price level.

$$\text{Real GDP} = \frac{\text{Nominal GDP}}{\text{GDP deflator}} \times 100$$

7. Conclusions. To accurately measure real output, it is necessary to use a price index to factor out any changes in prices hidden when examining nominal GDP alone.

   i. The GDP deflator is the price index used, since it measures changes in the prices of a wide range of both consumer and producer goods in an economy.

   ii. Once the deflator is calculated, a particular year's nominal GDP can be adjusted to reflect changes in the price level and then accurately expressed in constant dollars of the base year. In this way, a country can compare the real value of its national output from one year to the real GDP from another year.

   iii. In this case, one point of significance is that a recession, or significant slowdown of economic activity, is visible first in 2009 when looking only at nominal GDP. However, if real GDP is examined as well, one can observe this pattern by noting that real output actually declined from 2007 to 2008 even though nominal GDP rose by more than $300 billion.

Test Tip

Understanding the relationship between real GDP and nominal GDP will help you answer many multiple-choice questions. The AP exam tests your knowledge of this relationship in many ways. Here are two ways you might be asked about this relationship: 1) **If in a specified year nominal gross domestic product grew by 11 percent and real gross domestic product grew by 4 percent, how much is inflation?** *And,* 2) **Last year the GDP deflator rose from 150 to 156 and nominal GDP rose by 2%. By how much did real GDP change?**

8. The graphic below illustrates the process by which the nominal GDP of the United States is deflated to reflect changes in the prices level and to arrive at the real GDP figures for three years.

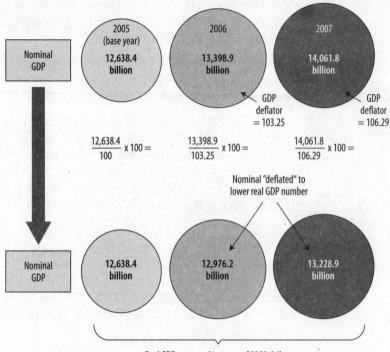

Real GDP expressed in terms of 2005 dollars

i. The light gray circles represent the nominal and real GDP in 2005, the base year. Since the GDP deflator is 100, the real and nominal GDP are the same.

ii. In 2006 and 2007, the nominal GDP, or the value of the total output of the United States expressed in terms of current dollars in the top row of circles, is in each case divided by the GDP deflator for that year to adjust the nominal GDP based on the change in the price level in order to arrive at the smaller bottom row of bubbles.

iii. In both 2006 and 2007, there is some inflation, evidenced by the rising price index.

iv. Inflation decreases the purchasing power of the dollar, so the dollar value of the output is deflated to the real GDP figure for every year following the base year.

v. The real GDP shows the value of the United States' output in 2006 and 2007 expressed in terms of 2005 dollars, meaning it shows what the nation's output in 2006 and 2007 would have been worth if the price level had remained as it was in 2005.

IV. Per Capita GDP

A. While real GDP adjusts for price changes, economists use another measure to adjust for population size.

B. Countries with large populations will necessarily have large economies since their supply of labor resources and human capital allows them to produce more output than countries with smaller populations.

C. To account for the average income in a nation, real GDP must be adjusted for the size of the population, yielding per capita GDP.

$$\text{Per Capita GDP} = \frac{\text{Real GDP}}{\text{Population}}$$

D. The countries with the largest economies are not always the richest countries on a per capita basis.

Countries with Largest GDP (trillions $ 2009)	Total GDP
1. United States	14.2
2. Japan	5.0
3. China	4.9
4. Germany	3.3
5. France	2.6

1. Japan and China have approximately equally sized economies at about $5 trillion per year. We could thus mistakenly infer that the Japanese and Chinese have roughly the equivalent material standard of living.

2. This conclusion would ignore the fact that China divides that income up between 1.3 billion more people, while Japan's population of 127 million is just one-tenth the size of China's.

3. With a nearly identical GDP, but a population 10 times larger, China's per capita income is just 10 percent that of Japan's, indicating the average Japanese person is 10 times richer than the average Chinese person.

E. Per capita GDP is the amount of national income divided by the population size.

1. It provides a far better sense of the approximate standard of living in a country than total GDP.

2. The table below once again shows the five largest countries by GDP, but in parentheses indicates their global ranking in terms of per capita GDP. In the right two columns are the top five countries in terms of per capita GDP, along with their average incomes.

Countries with Largest GDP (and Per Capita rank)	Total GDP (trillions $)	Country with Largest Per Capita GDP (and total GDP rank)	Per Capita GDP ($ in 2009)
1. United States (6)	14.2	1. Luxembourg (68)	105,350
2. Japan (14)	5.0	2. Norway (24)	79,089
3. China (86)	4.9	3. Denmark (29)	55,992
4. Germany (13)	3.3	4. Ireland (37)	51,049
5. France (12)	2.6	5. Netherlands (16)	47,917

3. Real GDP per capita gives us a better picture of how productive a country is on a per person basis.

4. While per capita GDP provides us more information about a country's economic performance and allows us to better compare incomes from one country to another, it tells us little about the income distribution within the country itself.

V. Economic Growth and Recession

A. *Economic growth* is defined as an increase in a nation's output of goods and services over a period of time.

B. *Recession* is defined as a significant decline in the economic activity spread across the country, lasting more than a few months, normally visible in real GDP growth, real personal income, employment, industrial production, and wholesale-retail sales.

C. A nation's economic growth rate is found by calculating the rate of change in real GDP from one period of time to the next.

$$\text{GDP Growth Rate} = \frac{\text{Real GDP in period 2} - \text{Real GDP in period 1}}{\text{Real GDP in period 1}} \times 100$$

1. Using the formula above, the GDP growth rate of the United States can be calculated for the years 2005–2009.

Year	Real GDP	Real GDP Growth Rate
2005	12,638.4	—
2006	12,976.2	$\frac{12,976.2 - 12,638.4}{12,638.4} \times 100 = 2.67\%$
2007	13,228.9	$\frac{13,228.9 - 12,976.2}{12,976.2} \times 100 = 1.95\%$
2008	13,228.8	$\frac{13,228.8 - 13,228.9}{13,228.9} \times 100 = 0.00\%$
2009	12,880.6	$\frac{12,880.6 - 13,228.8}{13,228.8} \times 100 = -2.63\%$

2. Between 2005 and 2007, the United States economy experienced positive economic growth. Each year, the real value of the nation's output increased from the previous year.

3. In 2008, the United States economy first stagnated (achieved no growth), and then entered recession

(experienced negative growth, or a decrease in the total output of goods and services).

D. Illustrating Economic Growth

1. Several macroeconomic models can be used to illustrate economic growth. The most basic method for showing growth is with the use of a production possibilities diagram. An outward shift of a nation's PPC shows that the nation is able to produce and consume more of everything.

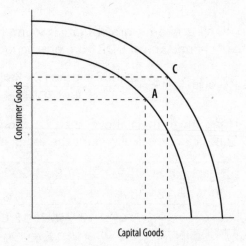

i. A shift from the inner curve to the outer curve in the graph above is possible only through an increase in the quality or quantity of the nation's productive resources.

ii. More capital, land, or labor, or better capital, land, or labor could lead to economic growth shown by an increase in a nation's production possibilities curve, allowing a country formerly operating at a point like A to now operate at a point like C, which previously would have been unattainable.

2. A second model that shows economic growth is the business cycle. The business cycle illustrates both short-run economic growth and long-run economic growth.

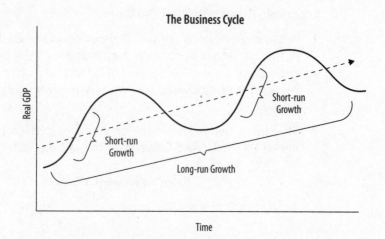

i. Due to the short-term fluctuations in consumption, investment, government spending, and net exports experienced as a normal part of a nation's business cycle, an economy may experience periods of rapid expansion followed by sudden contractions.

ii. The upward sloping sections of the business cycle represent periods of rapid short-run economic growth, or expansion phases of the business cycle.

iii. When the level of demand for a nation's output grows more rapidly than the level of aggregate supply, output may increase beyond the full-employment level in the short run.

iv. As wages and prices adjust to higher levels of demand, output will eventually fall and the period of rapid growth is followed by a recession, or contraction phase of the business cycle.

v. The slope of the "best fit" line on such a graph illustrates the economy's long-term growth rate.

The business cycle diagram, like the circular flow, is one that you will rarely be asked to draw. But you will often be asked questions about which phase of its business cycle a country is likely in given the existence of certain macroeconomic conditions, such as positive growth and low unemployment (expansion) or rising unemployment and deflation (contraction).

E. Economic Growth Around the World

1. While most nations continually seek to increase GDP, economic growth is not always a guarantee. As the business cycle diagram shows, periods of growth are often followed by periods of recession, followed by recovery and continued growth.

2. The graph below shows the economic growth rates experienced by the United States over the last eight decades.

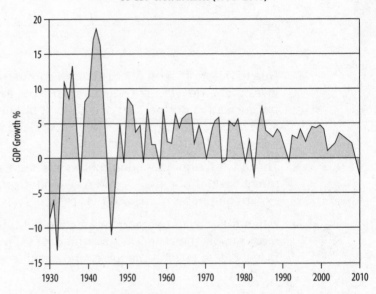

US GDP Growth Rates (1930–2010)

i. The years with the highest growth rates follow those in which the United States was in the deepest recession. These represent the periods of *recovery* in America's business cycle.

ii. Recessions have become less frequent and less intense in the decades since the Second World War.

iii. A better understanding of macroeconomic policy by the government and the central bank has helped smooth out the large fluctuations of the nineteenth and early twentieth centuries.

Inflation Measurement and Adjustment

I. Inflation and Deflation

A. *Inflation* is defined as an increase in the average price level of a nation's output over time.

1. If a nation is experiencing inflation, the inflation rate is positive.

2. Inflation rate is the percentage change in the price level between one period and a previous period. It can be determined using a price index.

B. *Deflation* is defined as a decrease in the average price level of a nation's output over time.

1. If a nation is experiencing deflation, the inflation rate is negative.

2. If the rate of inflation decreases between one period and the next but remains positive, then a nation is experiencing disinflation, not deflation.

C. Strengths of Inflation as a Macroeconomic Indicator

1. Inflation reduces the real incomes of the nation's households and therefore the standard of living of the nation's people.

2. Knowing the rate of change in the price level allows policymakers to implement appropriate policy responses to keep the price level relatively stable. Price-level stability is commonly considered an important goal of macroeconomic policy.

3. Deflation reduces the incentive for firms to invest in capital and employ workers.

4. If the economy is experiencing deflation, policymakers must be aware of this so they can implement policies to encourage consumption, investment, and employment.

D. Weaknesses of Inflation as a Macroeconomic Indicator

1. The inflation rate is based on a price index, which measures the changes in price of a particular selection of goods.

   i. If a particular household's typical consumption consists of goods that are not included in the price index, then inflation may not be a very accurate indicator of the changing costs of living for that household.

   ii. The basket of goods places weights on different categories of goods depending on the proportion of a typical household's budget that goes toward each category.

   ➤ For example, in the United States, food is weighted 15 percent, clothes 3.7 percent, and transportation 16.7 percent. Housing is weighted at 42 percent of the inflation measure in the United States.

   ➤ To households for whom housing and transportation make up a larger percentage of their monthly budget, an increase in home prices or rents may not be adequately reflected in the inflation figures, so inflation could understate the increases in living costs experienced by such families.

II. Measuring Inflation and Deflation— The Use of Price Indexes

A. A price index is a weighted average of prices. It tracks changes in the prices of a selection of the goods produced in a nation from one period of time to another.

1. When prices rise, the index number increases.

2. When prices fall, the index number decreases.

B. The Consumer Price Index (CPI) measures the prices of consumer goods and services and is widely used by governments to measure changes in the price level of the products that the typical household may buy in a particular time period.

1. The "basket of goods" measured for the CPI may include items such as clothing, food, fuel, electricity, rents, DVDs, airline tickets, bus fares, laptop computers, cellular phone service, and so on.

2. The "basket" measured by the CPI includes not only goods, but services, and its composition may be updated annually or biannually as new types of goods and services become fashionable among consumers.

   i. For instance, the CPI in the mid-90s would likely have included the price of musical compact discs.

   ii. Today's CPI may instead include the price of digital music downloads.

3. A price index is found by dividing the price of a basket of goods in one period by the price of the identical basket of goods in a base period and multiplying by 100. To determine the price index, first a base period index must be established.

4. For instance, assume the government wishes to determine how much prices have risen between July and August. The index for the base period of July (CPIj) is determined by

$$CPIj = \frac{Pbj}{Pbj} \times 100.$$

   i. Pbj is the price of a particular basket of goods in July. Since Pbj divided by Pbj equals one, the index for the base period (July) will be $1 \times 100 = 100$.

   ii. Now the price of the same basket of goods can be measured in August, and using this information we can determine the consumer price index for August (CPIa)

$$CPIa = \frac{Pba}{Pba} \times 100.$$

iii. As a simple demonstration, let us assume that only three goods are measured by a nation's CPI: pizza, haircuts, and wine, and that a typical household purchases one unit of each of the three goods per month. Study the table below and the calculation that follows.

Good or Service	Price in July	Price in August	Price in Sept.
Pizza	$10	$10.50	$10.50
Haircuts	$20	$19	$18
Wine	$8	$10	$10
Total basket price	$38	$39.50	$38.50
Price index	$\frac{38}{38} \times 100 = 100$	$\frac{39.5}{38} \times 100 = 104$	$\frac{38.5}{38} \times 100 = 101.3$

iv. Assume July is the base period. To calculate the CPI for August (CPIa), we take the price of the basket of goods in August and divide it by the price of the same basket of goods in July and multiply the result by 100:
$$\frac{39.5}{38} \times 100 = 104.$$

v. An increase in a price index such as in our example above indicates that the average price level has risen.

vi. An increase in the price index from 100 to 104 indicates that a basket of goods that would have cost $100 in July would cost $104 in August.

vii. The purchasing power of the dollar decreased and the economy experienced inflation between July and August.

5. The price index for September (CPIs) with the base period remaining July is $\frac{38.5}{38} \times 100 = 101.3$.

   i.   The price index in September indicates that the average price level decreased from August, but was still higher than in July.

   ii. The economy experienced deflation (a decrease in the average price level) between August and September. But using July as the base period, the price level is higher overall in September.

   iii. A basket of goods that would have cost $104 in August now costs only $101.3 in September.

   iv. The purchasing power of the dollar increased between August and September, but the dollar still buys less in September than it would have in July, since the basket of goods costing $100 in July cost $101.3 in September.

6. An actual consumer price index includes hundreds of goods and services of various types, not just three as in our example. But the interpretation of the results is the same regardless of how many products make up the basket of goods.

III. Calculating the Inflation Rate Using the CPI

A. The inflation rate is the percentage change in the average price of goods and services over time.

B. To calculate the inflation rate between two periods of time, the percentage change in the price index must be determined.

1. The inflation rate (IR) between two periods of time is determined using the following formula: $IR = \dfrac{CPI2 - CPI1}{CPI1} \times 100$.

2. In our example above, the inflation rate between July and August is: $\dfrac{104 - 100}{100} \times 100 = 4\%$.

   i.   The average price of goods in the nation is four percent higher in August than in July.

   ii. The country experienced inflation.

      iii. The purchasing power of the dollar is weaker in August than in July, since it takes more dollars to buy the same basket of goods now than when it was bought in July.

3. Between August and September *inflation* is

$$\frac{101.3 - 104}{104} \times 100 = -2.5\%.$$

      i. The average price of goods in the nation is 2.59 percent lower.

      ii. The country experienced deflation.

      iii. The purchasing power of the dollar is stronger in September than in August, since it now takes fewer dollars to buy the same basket of goods now than when it was bought in August.

C. Weighted Categories in the CPI

1. To account for the different proportions of a typical household's disposable income that goes toward the purchase of different types of goods, a government will assign weights to categories of goods measured in the CPI.

      i. The total weight of all categories must add up to 100. The weight of any individual category reflects the relative importance to households.

      ii. Weighting categories assures that when a particular category of good experiences large fluctuations in price over time, the overall CPI does not fluctuate wildly, rather it adjusts in a manner that reflects the impact that price changes in that particular category have on the typical consumer's cost of living. For example, because Americans spend more of their income on gasoline than on paper clips, changes in the price of gasoline affect the CPI more than changes in the price of paper clips.

      iii. The table below shows how the United States Bureau of Labor Statistics weights different categories of goods when measuring inflation.[2]

---

[2] Source: *http://www.bls.gov.*

Category	Weight
Food and beverages	14.795
Housing	41.96
Apparel	3.695
Transportation	16.685
Medical care	6.513
Recreation	6.437
Education and communication	6.434
Other goods and services	3.483
Total	100

2. Based on the category weights above, we can estimate the effect a change in the price of goods in a particular category will have on the overall inflation figure in the United States.

3. For instance, assume rising food prices cause the average price in the "food and beverages" category to increase by five percent in a given year.

4. The "food and beverages" category accounts for just 14.795 percent of the total CPI. To determine the effect this has on overall inflation, we must multiply the change in category price (PC) by the category weight, expressed as a decimal.

   i. %ΔCPI = %ΔPC (Weight × 0.01).

   ii. When food prices rise by five percent, the effect on the CPI will be: 5%(14.795 × 0.01) = 0.74%.

   iii. A five percent increase in food prices will cause inflation to rise by 0.74 percent.

5. In this way, inflation provides a more accurate reflection of the real cost of living.

   i. If the average price of goods in a relatively unimportant category (such as recreation) rises or falls dramatically, the overall inflation rate will adjust only minimally.

   ii. But if the prices in more important categories, such as housing, change dramatically, the inflation rate will adjust more noticeably.

D. Other Price Indexes

1. Besides the Consumer Price Index, there are two others regularly used by the United States government.

   i. The Producer Price Index (PPI) measures the change in the prices received by domestic producers. It is also called the Wholesale Price Index.

      ➤ Differs from the CPI in that it measures the price level from producers' perspectives, not consumers.

      ➤ The PPI takes into account factors such as government subsidies, distribution costs, sales, and excise taxes.

   ii. Gross Domestic Product Deflator measures of the level of prices of all new, domestically produced final goods and services in an economy.

      ➤ The GDP deflator is the broadest measure of inflation, as it includes both producer and consumer goods.

      ➤ It is used to adjust a nation's nominal GDP for changes in the price level.

IV. The Costs of Inflation

A. Loss of Purchasing Power

1. Inflation erodes the purchasing power of a household's income.

2. Just as a high inflation rate will "deflate" national income, it also reduces real household income.

3. The real income (Ir) of a household is found by dividing its nominal income (In) by the CPI expressed in hundredths:

$$IR = \frac{In}{CPI \times 0.01}.$$

i. For example, if a household earns a nominal income in 2011 of $55,000, and the CPI for that year is 108.5 (with a base year of 2005), then the household's real income is $\dfrac{55,000}{108.5 \times 0.01} = 50,691$.

ii. The household's real income is lower than if inflation had been less between 2005 and 2011.

➤ If the CPI had been only 105 in 2011, then the household's real income would have been $\dfrac{55,000}{105 \times 0.01} = 52,380$.

➤ Because of inflation, if nominal income remains unchanged, the real income of households is lower year after year.

➤ If nominal income grows at a slower rate than the price level, than households will grow poorer in real terms over time.

B. Lower Real Interest Rates for Savers

1. Just as unanticipated inflation reduces real incomes, it also reduces the real interest rates earned by people saving money in banks.

2. An interest rate is the return on savings. Money saved in a bank grows each year by the amount of interest earned.

3. If there is inflation that was unanticipated by the bank, then the real interest rate (ir_r) will be lower than the nominal interest rate (ir_n) by the rate of inflation.

i. $ir_r = ir_n -$ inflation rate

ii. For example, if you have money in a bank earning five percent interest, and there is unanticipated inflation of three percent, then the real interest rate (actual increase in purchasing power) you are earning is only two percent.

iii. For every $100 you have in the bank, you will earn $5 per year in interest. But since price levels are three percent higher at the end of the year, you can buy only two percent more stuff with your $5 of interest earned.

iv. On the other hand, borrowers might benefit from this unanticipated inflation because they would be able to pay off their debts in dollars that are each worth less purchasing power.

C. Higher Nominal Interest Rates for Borrowers if Inflation Is Anticipated

1. The interest rate is also the cost of borrowing money and is based on estimations the lender makes about two things: the riskiness of lending to that borrower and the price level at the time of repayment.

2. If banks anticipate inflation, they will charge higher interest rates to borrowers.

3. The nominal interest rate banks charge borrowers typically includes an inflation premium, based on the expected rate of inflation.

4. If inflation is expected in the next year, banks will charge a higher rate to borrowers to adjust for the reduced value of the money being repaid by the household or firm borrowing the money.

5. The nominal interest rate banks charge equals the desired real interest rate plus an inflation premium based on the level of inflation anticipated.

i. For instance, if a bank wants to make a loan to a borrower at a real rate of 6 percent, but there is expected inflation of 5 percent, then the bank will charge the borrower a nominal rate of 11 percent.

ii. At lower rates of expected inflation, borrowers will enjoy lower interest rates. If inflation were expected to be only two percent, then the nominal rate paid by the firm borrowing money would be only eight percent.

    iii. Lower inflation makes it cheaper for firms to borrow money to invest in capital, allowing for more job creation.

D. Inflationary Spirals

  1. If there is inflation in an economy, firms and households will prefer to spend their money now rather than save.

  2. High unanticipated inflation reduces the incentive to save, since it lowers the real interest rate.

  3. More spending in the economy contributes to more inflation. Over time, workers will begin to demand higher wages, which further contributes to inflation.

  4. An inflationary spiral is when higher prices lead to more spending, which leads to even higher prices and demands among workers for higher wages, contributing to even more inflation.

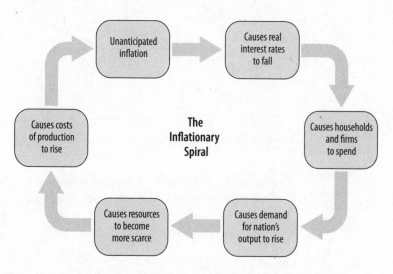

E. The Importance of Keeping Inflation Under Control

  1. Most central banks and governments target inflation at around two to three percent. Anything less than that may cause the fear of deflation. Anything greater than that may

lead producers and consumers to act in ways that increase the odds of the inflationary spiral shown above.

2. Fiscal, monetary, and supply-side policies may be implemented to keep the level of inflation low and stable.

Knowing who benefits and who suffers from inflation is important. The AP exam often asks questions about the effects of unanticipated inflation on savers, borrowers, creditors, and so on, to see if you understand how rising prices affect real interest rates.

Unemployment

I. Employment and Unemployment

A. *Unemployment* means to be actively seeking, but unable to find, work.

B. *Employment* means to have a paid job, either part time or full time, of any type.

C. The *unemployment rate* is the percentage of the labor force that is unemployed.

1. The labor force is the non-institutionalized population of a nation between the ages of 16 and 64 that are either employed or unemployed.

2. Each of the following people are part of the labor force because they are either employed or unemployed:

    i. A part-time retail-sales clerk who is also going to college is part of the labor force because she is employed.

    ii. A full-time nurse is part of the labor force because he is employed.

    iii. A factory worker whose plant closed and who is applying for jobs at other factories is part of the labor force because he is unemployed.

    iv. A recent college graduate interviewing at different companies for her first job is part of the labor force because she is unemployed.

3. Examples of people *not* in the labor force:

    i. A stay-at-home mother is not part of the labor force because she is not employed or seeking employment.

    ii. A college graduate who volunteers in a community center is not part of the labor force because, while he is working, he is not formally employed nor is he seeking employment.

    iii. A discouraged worker who has been looking for a job for 18 months but has given up the job search is not part of the labor force because he is no longer actively seeking employment.

    iv. An engineer who quits his job and goes back to school to earn a teaching degree is not part of the labor force because he is not currently employed or seeking employment.

4. Measuring the unemployment rate:

    i. $$\text{Unemployment Rate} = \frac{\text{Number of people unemployed}}{\text{Number of people in the labor force}} \times 100$$

    ii. Assume the following about the labor force in the United States:

      ➤ There are 14 million people out of work and actively seeking jobs.

      ➤ There are 126 million people employed either part time or full time.

      ➤ The labor force = 14 million unemployed + 126 million employed Americans = 140 million people.

      ➤ The unemployment rate $= \dfrac{14 \text{ million unemployed}}{140 \text{ million in the labor force}}$

        $= 0.1 \times 100 = 10\%$

5. Unemployment rises during recessions and falls during expansionary phases of the business cycle.

i. During the United States recession of 2008 and 2009, the unemployment rate rose, as the demand for labor to produce goods and services fell.

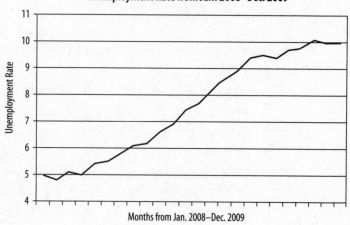

Unemployment Rate from Jan. 2008–Dec. 2009

Months from Jan. 2008–Dec. 2009

ii. During periods of rapid economic growth, the unemployment rate falls, as seen between 1992 and 2000 in the graph below.

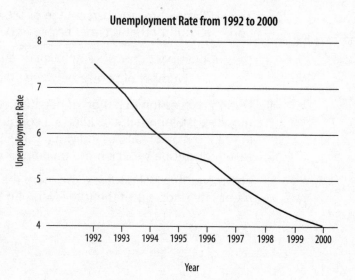

Unemployment Rate from 1992 to 2000

Year

D. The unemployment rate is one of the major indicators of economic well-being because it shows the degree to which a society is using its available labor resources, which in turn reveals how closely society is approaching its potential output or PPC. However, the unemployment rate is not a perfect indication of an economy's health.

E. Shortcomings of the unemployment rate as a measure of economic well-being:

1. Unemployment does not include discouraged workers.

   i. A *discouraged worker* is a worker who has been unemployed for a period of time and has given up the search for a job.

   ii. Such a worker is not considered part of the labor force, so is not included in the nation's unemployment figures.

   iii. Because they are not counted, the unemployment rate may understate how bad things are during long recessions, which create lots of discouraged workers.

2. Labor force participation rate (LFPR) decreases during a recession.

   i. The LFPR measures the percentage of the adult population in a country that is either employed or unemployed.

   ii. $\text{LFPR} = \dfrac{\text{Number of people employed or unemployed}}{\text{Number of people between 16 and 64}}$

   iii. During a recession (a period of negative economic growth), the number of adults in a country participating in the job market falls, as individuals give up on the job search or decide to seek more training or education.

   iv. The more the LFPR declines, the more the unemployment rate understates the true levels of unemployment.

> For the AP exam, you should to be able to calculate the unemployment rate from a set of data. For example, a question may say: Assume in a hypothetical economy the following: 800 people are employed full time, 150 people are employed part time, 50 people are unemployed, and 50 people are discouraged workers and have given up on the job search. What is the unemployment rate? *This problem requires not only a simple calculation, but also the definition of unemployment, discouraged workers, and knowledge of who is considered employed. If you know all this, you can conclude that the unemployment rate is 50/1,000 = 0.05 x 100 = 5%.*

II. Types of Unemployment

A. An unemployed person is someone who is willing and able to work, but unable to find a job. There are several categories of unemployment. The category under which a particular unemployed person falls depends upon his or her characteristics.

B. Frictional Unemployment. Someone is frictionally unemployed if he or she is "in between jobs" or seeking his or her first job but has employable skills.

1. Examples of frictionally unemployed individuals include:

   i. A college graduate who is entering the job market for the first time.

   ii. A professional accountant who leaves his job in Chicago to move to Boston, and is looking for a new job as an accountant there.

   iii. A teacher who resigns from one school and begins looking for a better-paying job at another school.

2. During the period in between one job and another, a worker is frictionally unemployed because workers and firms for which they are a good fit have yet to find one another.

3. One important characteristic of frictional unemployment is that the individuals all possess skills that are in demand in the nation's economy, and therefore are likely to gain employment in a reasonably short period of time.

4. Frictional unemployment is considered natural unemployment because its existence is evidence that:

    i. The economy is doing well enough that people feel they are able to quit a job and look for another job.

    ii. The ability of people with skills that are in demand and who are looking for work allows an economy to grow in the short run.

    iii. Firms find it reasonably easy to hire skilled, able workers when there is some level of frictional unemployment in the economy because useful and well-trained workers are available for hire.

C. Structural Unemployment. Workers are structurally unemployed when they lose their jobs to a changing structure of the economy (i.e., their skills are no longer in demand by the nation's producers).

1. Examples of structurally unemployed individuals include:

    i. An automobile factory worker who is laid off because the company has acquired a machine that does the particular task he had been trained to do.

    ii. A worker in a tire factory who loses his job because the factory has moved its manufacturing to Mexico.

    iii. A teacher who loses his job because the school district, in an effort to save money, has decided to offer classes online, which allows one teacher to teach twice as many students as before.

    iv. In all of the above examples, the workers have lost their jobs due to either improvements in technology or due to the globalization of their industries—changes in the structure of the economy that render some types of workers no longer necessary.

2. Workers who are structurally unemployed are likely to remain that way for a longer period of time than those who

are frictionally unemployed, because they do not possess skills that are currently in demand in the nation's economy. Ways to reduce structural unemployment include:

i.   Re-training of unemployed workers;

ii. Better education;

iii. More wage flexibility (firms are less likely to replace workers with technology if workers' wages are more flexible).

3. Structural unemployment, like frictional, is considered natural unemployment, since its existence is evidence of a healthy economy in which overall output and productivity is likely growing. For instance:

i.   The automobile factory is likely to produce more cars at a lower cost by employing more technology and less labor.

ii. The tire factory is able to produce tires more cheaply, lowering their price to consumers and increasing the quantity available, by producing in Mexico instead of the United States.

iii. The school district requires less taxpayer money when offering classes online than in smaller, more costly face-to-face classrooms.

D. Cyclical Unemployment. Cyclical unemployment results from a fall in total demand for a nation's output. It is associated with the recession or contraction phase of the nation's business cycle.

1. Examples of cyclically unemployed individuals include:

i.   A bank's loan manager who is let go because there is a fall in demand for bank loans from households and firms.

ii. A clerk at an electronics store who is laid off because sales of consumer electronics have fallen.

iii. A massage therapist whose business fails because fewer people demand these types of services when their incomes are down.

2. In each of the examples above, unemployment is caused by a fall in the demand for particular goods and services.

3. Cyclical unemployment, unlike frictional and structural unemployment, is not considered natural, because when an economy is producing at or near its full employment level there is a high overall demand for goods and services and therefore people with relevant skills find it easy to find employment. In these circumstances cyclical unemployment would be close to zero.

4. Cyclically unemployed individuals generally possess the skills demanded in the economy, but since overall demand is low, they find themselves out of a job.

5. Ways to reduce cyclical unemployment include:

    i. Cutting taxes for households, which increases consumption, increasing demand for labor.

    ii. Increasing government spending, which creates demand for all sorts of goods and services, putting cyclically unemployed workers back to work.

    iii. Lowering interest rates, which stimulates new investment in capital by firms, hopefully increasing demand for labor.

    iv. Depreciating the nation's currency, which increases demand for exports from abroad and for workers to produce those exports.

6. The above solutions to cyclical unemployment will be explained further in later chapters. However, all are examples of expansionary policies designed to put more people to work.

Test Tip

Be able to determine what type of unemployment someone is experiencing based on a description. The AP exam may state, James has just finished school and is looking for his first job. James is . . . and then let you choose from the different types of unemployment. You must be able to conclude that James is frictionally unemployed. Other examples of cyclical and structural unemployment may be given to test whether you can distinguish between the types of unemployment.

III. The Natural Rate of Unemployment (NRU)

A. The NRU is the level of unemployment that prevails when an economy is producing at its full-employment level.

B. An economy producing at full employment (shown on the PPC as a point just inside the curve) experiences only frictional and structural unemployment.

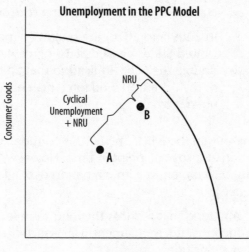

Unemployment in the PPC Model

1. In the graph above, point B corresponds with the nation's full employment level of output.

   i. Unemployment in the economy includes only frictional and structural unemployment.

   ii. The unemployment rate at point B is *the natural rate of unemployment*.

   iii. In the United States, the NRU is generally thought to be between four percent and six percent.

   iv. When the United States economy is "healthy," somewhere around five percent of the labor force should be unemployed.

2. Point A in the graph above represents the level of output during a recession.

   i. Unemployment in the economy includes frictional, structural, and cyclical unemployment.

   ii. The unemployment rate at point A is greater than the natural rate of unemployment.

   iii. If overall demand for goods and services falls in a country, unemployment will grow beyond the natural rate, and the economy will enter a recession.

   iv. In 2009 and 2010, the unemployment rate in the United States peaked at 10 percent, approximately double the NRU, indicating that an additional 5 percent of the American workforce may have been cyclically unemployed.

C. Changes in the NRU. The NRU is considered to be stable in a nation at a specific point in time. However, it can vary from nation to nation or within a nation over a longer period of years or decades.

   1. Anything that reduces the long-term level of structural or frictional unemployment will reduce the nation's NRU. These may include:

      i. Programs or services that match skilled workers with employers.

      ii. Job training programs that give structurally unemployed workers skills to get them back to work quickly in the changing economy.

      iii. Reducing or shortening the period of time over which unemployed workers may receive government benefits. This creates the incentive for workers to accept jobs at lower wage rates and remain unemployed for a shorter period of time.

      iv. Reduction in trade union power. Unions bargain for higher wages and more benefits for employees, which means firms must reduce the size of their workforce to keep costs low. Less union power should increase the supply of labor and reduce the level of structural unemployment.

    v.   Reduction in the minimum wage. A lower or no minimum wage will allow firms to employ more workers even when the economy is producing at its full-employment level, reducing the NRU.

  2. Different countries have different natural rates of unemployment depending on the characteristics of each country.

The NRU exists when an economy is at its full-employment level of output. This is a major point of confusion for students, who often mistakenly assume that full employment corresponds with zero percent unemployment. This is incorrect; in fact, the NRU is the desired level of unemployment in an economy, since having some unemployed workers leaves the economy room to grow in the short run.

IV. The Costs of Unemployment

A. The existence of unemployment in a country has several economic and social consequences.

  1. Individual Consequences of Unemployment

    i.   Decreased household income and purchasing power. A household in which one or more individuals is unemployed must live on a lower level of income, reducing its standard of living.

    ii. Increased levels of psychological and physical illness. Studies have shown that unemployment leads to more mental illness and even higher suicide rates.

  2. Social Consequences of Unemployment

    i.   Downward pressure on wages for the employed. A large pool of unemployed workers increases the likelihood that those who still have a job will have to take pay cuts or risk losing their jobs too.

    ii.   Increased poverty and crime. Unemployed individuals are more likely to turn to crime or end up in poverty.

    iii.   Transformation of traditional societies. Unemployment in rural areas in the developing world has led to migrations and the disintegration of traditional society.

3. Economic Consequences of Unemployment

    i.   Lower level of aggregate demand. Workers without jobs consume fewer goods and services, meaning even more workers will lose their jobs.

    ii.   Underutilization of the nation's resources. The higher the level of unemployment, the greater the gap between the nation's actual output and its potential output, meaning less income for the average household.

    iii.   "Brain drain." Skilled workers may choose to leave a country with high unemployment if job opportunities are more abundant elsewhere.

    iv.   A turn toward protectionism and isolationist policies. Governments may try to "protect" workers by creating barriers to trade with the rest of the world.

    v.   Increased budget deficits. High unemployment reduces tax revenues flowing to a government while increasing public expenditures on financial support for the unemployed.

B. Due to the multiple economic and social costs of unemployment, governments and policymakers have made it a priority to promote the achievement of full employment.

PART IV

NATIONAL INCOME AND PRICE DETERMINATION

Aggregate Demand

I. Aggregate Demand

A. *Aggregate demand* is the function relating price level and the amount of output of a nation demanded in a given period of time.

1. Unlike "demand," which represents the willingness and ability of consumers to buy a particular good or service, aggregate demand aggregates the demands of all consumers for all the goods and services produced in a nation in a given time period at different price levels.

2. There is an inverse relationship between the quantity of real output demanded and the price level, meaning that at lower price levels there is a greater amount of output demanded and at higher price levels the amount of output demanded decreases.

3. Aggregate demand measures the demand for a nation's output of goods and services in a year, or its Gross Domestic Product (GDP). It bears a close relationship to the expenditure method of GDP.

B. Aggregate demand for a nation's output consists of four distinct types of spending:

1. Consumption (C) includes all spending by domestic households on goods and services.

2. Investment (I) measures the total spending by firms on capital equipment and by households on real estate or homes.

3. Government spending (G) measures a country's government's expenditures on goods and services.

4. Net exports (Xn or X – M) measures the total income earned from the sale of exports (X) to foreigners minus the total amount spent by a nation's households, firms, and government on goods and services imported (M) from other countries.

C. The Aggregate Demand Curve. The total demand for a nation's output is represented by a downward sloping curve, inversely related to the average price level.

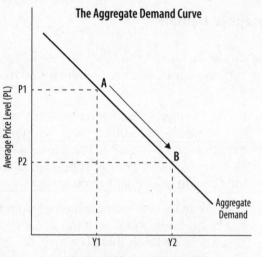

The Aggregate Demand Curve

Real National Output and Income (rGDP)

1. There are three explanations for the inverse relationship between the average price level (PL) and real national output (rGDP):

   i.   The Wealth Effect. Higher price levels reduce the purchasing power or the real value of the nation's households' wealth and savings. The public feels poorer at higher price levels and thus demands a lower quantity of the nation's output when price levels are high.

   ii. The Interest Rate Effect. In response to a rise in the price level, banks will raise the interest rates on loans to households and firms that wish to consume or invest. At higher interest rates, the quantity demanded of products and capital for which households and firms must borrow decreases, as borrowers find higher interest rates less attractive.

   iii. The Net Export Effect. As the price level in a particular country rises, *ceteris paribus* (other things being equal), goods and services produced in that country become less attractive to foreign consumers, and imports become more attractive to domestic consumers. Therefore, at higher average price levels, less of the nation's output is demanded than at lower price levels.

2. A change in the price level of a nation's output (which itself could result from a shift in aggregate supply) will lead to a movement along the AD curve and a change in the quantity of national output demanded.

D. Shifts in the AD Curve

1. A change in any of the non-price level determinants of aggregate demand will cause a shift in the AD curve.

2. AD will increase and shift to the right if consumption, investment, government spending, or net exports increase.

3. AD will decrease and shift to the left if C, I, G, or Xn decrease.

Understanding how changes in various factors will affect aggregate demand is very important. For example, you must know how lower interest rates will affect each of the components of AD, and how expectations of higher inflation will affect consumer and firm behavior. Expect several questions in the multiple-choice section on changes to such variables.

II. The Components of Aggregate Demand

A. Consumption. Consumption includes all purchases of durable and non-durable goods and services by domestic households.

1. Consumption makes up the largest proportion of aggregate demand in the United States, equaling more than 60 percent of the nation's GDP in 2009.

2. In some countries, usually those in which tax rates are higher than in the United States (such as Sweden, Denmark, France, and Germany), consumption makes up a smaller proportion of total GDP, equaling just 30 percent in Sweden, for instance.

3. Determinants of Consumption. The level of household consumption in any country depends upon several variables:

   i. The level of income determines the level of consumption.

      ➤ At higher income levels, household consumption rises.

      ➤ As national income rises, consumption rises, since there is more income to be spent on goods and services.

      ➤ As national income falls, consumption falls, since there is less household income generated to pay for consumption.

   ii. Average propensities to consume and save.

      ➤ At low-income levels, the average propensity to consume (APC) is high. This is the proportion of national income that goes toward consumption.

      ➤ The average propensity to save is very low at low-income levels, since very little money is left for households to save once their necessities are purchased.

$$APC = \frac{Consumption\ (C)}{Income\ (Y)}$$

$$APS = \frac{Savings\ (S)}{Income\ (Y)}$$

$$APC + APS = 1$$

      ➤ As income rises, the average propensity to consume falls, since higher-income households are able to save more of their total income. The average propensity to save increases as income increases.

iii. Marginal propensities to consume and save.

➤ The marginal propensity to consume (MPC) is the change in consumption that results from a particular change in income.
$$MPC = \frac{\text{Change in consumption } (\Delta C)}{\text{Change in income } (\Delta Y)}.$$

— For example, if national income rises by $5 billion and consumption increases by $3 billion, then $MPC = \frac{\Delta C}{\Delta Y} = \frac{3}{5} = 0.6$.

— This means that 60 percent of any increase in national income will go toward domestic consumption.

➤ The marginal propensity to save (MPS) is the change in savings that results from a particular change in income. $MPS = \frac{\text{Change in savings } (\Delta S)}{\text{Change in income } (\Delta Y)}$

— For example, if the same increase in national income of $5 billion described above leads to an increase in savings of only $2 billion, then the $MPS = \frac{\Delta S}{\Delta Y} = \frac{2}{5} = 0.4$.

— This means that 40 percent of any increase in national income will go toward savings, a *leakage* from the circular flow of income.

➤ The MPC and the MPS together will always equal ONE in a private closed economy, because new disposable income must be either spent or saved. $MPC + MPS = 1$.

➤ The MPC and MPS are useful in determining the effect any change in expenditures (such as an increase in government spending or investment) will have on the nation's GDP.

iv. Wealth determines the level of consumption.

> ➤ Household wealth is the value of a household's assets minus all its liabilities. Households' assets may include real estate, stocks, bonds, savings accounts, mutual funds, etc.

> ➤ When asset prices rise, households *feel richer* and tend to consume more at each level of income.

> ➤ When asset prices fall, households consume less at each level of income.

> ➤ The fact that wealth determines consumption explains why changes in the value of the stock market or real estate have such dramatic effects on the level of economic activity in a nation.

>> — A change in the value of the stock market itself has no effect on aggregate demand, but since stocks are an important component of wealth, consumption is affected when stocks rise or fall.

>> — A change in the value of real estate has no immediate effect on AD, but since homes are an important asset for households, real estate prices have a major effect on the level of consumption and therefore AD.

v. Interest rates determine the level of consumption.

> ➤ A change in interest rates (the opportunity cost of money) affects consumption.

>> — At higher interest rates, households prefer to save more and consume less.

>> — At lower interest rates, it becomes cheaper to borrow money to consume, and there is a lower return on savings, so consumption rises and savings falls.

vi. Consumer expectations determine the level of consumption.

➤ If households are hopeful about future employment and income opportunities, they will be more likely to consume at their current level of income. During periods of economic growth, confidence tends to be high and consumption rises.

➤ If households are pessimistic about the future, consumption tends to fall and savings increase.

B. Investment. Investment includes the purchase of capital goods by firms and the purchase of newly-constructed homes by households.

1. In 2009 investment made up approximately 12 percent of the total spending on goods and services in the United States.

2. In developing economies, investment typically makes up a larger proportion of total demand than in more developed economies. This is explained by the fact that less-developed countries have a lower capital to labor ratio, meaning that they are starting from a level of development at which workers have less capital. Investment increases the level of capital in an economy and contributes to the level of economic growth.

3. The level of investment in an economy is dependent on the following determinants:

   i. Interest rates determine the level of investment.

      ➤ At higher interest rates, firms find it more costly to borrow the funds needed to acquire new capital.

      ➤ At lower interest rates, firms will find more investment projects whose expected rates of return exceed the level of interest and therefore are seen as profitable investments.

      ➤ There is an inverse relationship between the interest rate in a nation and the quantity of funds demanded for investment, as seen in the Investment Demand diagram:

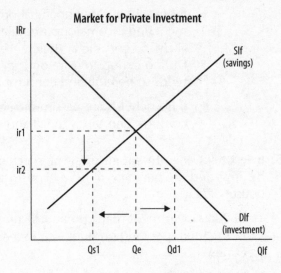

Market for Private Investment

- In the Market for Private Investment, there is an inverse relationship between the real interest rate and the demand for funds for investment.

- There is a direct relationship between the real interest rate and the supply of funds available for investment, since households and firms will save more money at higher interest rates.

➤ At ir1, the quantity of funds available for private investment equals the quantity demanded.

➤ At ir2, the quantity demanded for investment increases to Qd1, since more investments will have expected rates of return equal to or greater than ir2.

➤ At ir2, the quantity supplied of funds for investment is only Qs1, since the return on savings is lower and households find it more desirable to consume than to save.

➤ Since investment is highly sensitive to the interest rate, macroeconomic policies that can affect the interest rate (monetary policy) can stimulate or contract the level of private investment in the economy.

ii. Investment is determined by the level of business confidence and expectations.

➤ If firms expect business conditions and consumer demand to be strong in the future, the Investment Demand Curve (DIf) will increase and shift to the right.

➤ If firms expect prices to rise in the future (inflation), they will wish to invest in more capital now to meet the rising demand for their products.

➤ If firms' expectations are poor, the demand for investment will decrease now, shifting DIf to the left.

➤ If firms expect the price level to fall or consumer demand to decline in the future, they will demand less funds for investment now.

iii. Investment demand is determined by technology.

➤ New technologies (such as the Internet, alternative energies, mobile computing) lead to an increase in demand for funds for investment now.

➤ Technological change is the result of investment, but also leads to further increases in investment.

iv. Investment demand is determined by the level of government regulation and business taxes.

➤ Lower taxes and fewer regulations by the government increase demand for investment by firms.

➤ Higher taxes on capital gains or profits and burdensome regulations on firms' behavior reduce the level of private investment demand.

4. Investment is a very important determinant of the level of economic growth in a nation. Policies that encourage private investment can lead to more employment and long-run economic growth because they increase the nation's capital stock.

The Investment Demand diagram is very similar to, and can be used interchangeably with, the Loanable Funds diagram. Both show the relationship between the interest rate and the quantity of investment in an economy.

C. Government Spending. Government spending includes all spending on goods and services by the government. This includes public goods such as infrastructure and national defense and the provision of subsidies to firms. It excludes transfer payments, such as unemployment benefits and Social Security, as these simply transfer income from one group of people to another.

1. In 2009 government spending accounted for roughly 35 percent of the total demand for goods and services in the United States.

2. Government spending makes up a larger proportion of GDP during recessions, as *fiscal policies* are implemented to offset falls in private demand (see Chapter 12).

3. Government spending is financed by:

    i. Taxes paid by the country's households and firms;

    ii. Debt. Any spending by government that exceeds the tax revenues collected must be paid for by the issue of government bonds, or certificates of debt;

    iii. A combination of taxes and debt. The national debt is the sum of a country's past annual deficits. The greater the difference between a government's budget and its tax revenues in a given year, the larger the annual deficit, which adds to the national debt.

4. Government spending is determined primarily by the level of private aggregate demand in the nation and a government's *fiscal policy*.

    i. When an economy is growing and producing at or near full employment, government spending can be decreased as there is less need for a large government sector in a healthy economy. A decrease in government spending (or an increase in taxes) when an economy is at or beyond full employment is called contractionary fiscal policy.

ii. When an economy is in recession, government spending tends to increase as the government finds it necessary to fill the recessionary gap (the gap in output between the recessionary level and the level of full employment output.) An increase in government spending (or a decrease in taxes) when an economy is in recession is called expansionary fiscal policy.

D. Net Exports. Net exports measure the total revenue earned by a nation's exports minus the nation's total spending on imports. Money earned from exports is an injection into the circular flow and therefore contributes to aggregate demand, while money spent on imports is a leakage and therefore is subtracted from aggregate demand.

1. Net exports actually accounted for a negative three percent of the total demand for goods and services in the United States in 2009, meaning the United States had a net deficit in its balance of trade, or current account, with the rest of the world.

    i. If a country earns more from exports than it spends on imports, it has a trade surplus.

    ii. If a country spends more on imports than it earns from exports, it has a trade deficit (see Chapter 15).

2. The primary determinants of a country's net exports are:

    i. Foreign consumers' tastes and preferences. If foreigners demand more of a nation's goods, then the nation's net exports will rise.

    ii. Foreign consumers' income. If incomes abroad rise, then demand for a nation's output should rise as foreigners buy more imported goods and services.

    iii. Exchange rates (see Chapter 16). The exchange rate is the price of a nation's currency in terms of another nation's currency.

➤ If a country's currency becomes stronger relative to its trading partners' currencies, then its exports appear more expensive and demand should fall, lowering net exports.

➤ If a country's currency weakens relative to other countries' currencies, its exports appear cheaper and demand should rise, increasing net exports.

iv. Protectionism. *Protectionism* refers to the use of government policies aimed at reducing the level of imported goods and services to protect domestic producers.

➤ High taxes on imported goods and services (called tariffs) reduce demand for imports in a nation, increasing the country's net exports.

➤ Subsidies for domestic producers of exported goods and services will make them cheaper abroad, increasing demand abroad and the nation's net exports.

➤ Quotas are physical limits on the number of a particular good allowed to be imported. Imposing quotas on imports can reduce the number of imported goods and increase a nation's net exports.

➤ Most economists believe that protectionism tends to reduce the benefits of trading, because fewer chances to reduce opportunity costs are realized.

III. The Multiplier Effect and the Crowding-Out Effect

A. The Multiplier Effect. Whenever any one of the components of AD increases (C, I, G, or Xn), the ultimate increase in GDP will be greater than the initial increase in expenditures.

1. The impact on GDP of a particular increase in spending in an economy depends on the proportion of the new income that is *leaked* relative to the proportion that continues to circulate in the economy.

2. The multiplier effect tells us the impact a particular change in one of the components of AD will have on the total income and output (GDP). The spending multiplier (k) is a function of the marginal propensity to consume and save in a nation (MPC and MPS).

   i. The spending multiplier (k) equals $\dfrac{1}{MPS}$ or $\dfrac{1}{1-MPC}$.

   ii. The larger the marginal propensity to consume in a nation, the larger the spending multiplier will be.

   ➤ Assume that Americans spend 80 percent of any increase in income they experience, and save only 20 percent. The spending multiplier is $k = \dfrac{1}{1-0.8} = \dfrac{1}{0.2} = 5$. A $10 billion increase in G, I, or Xn will lead to a $50 billion increase in GDP.

   ➤ Now assume Americans spend only 50 percent of any increase in income, and save 50 percent. The spending multiplier is $k = \dfrac{1}{1-0.5} = \dfrac{1}{0.5} = 2$. A $10 billion increase in G, I, or Xn will lead to a $20 billion increase in GDP.

   ➤ Notice that the larger the MPC, the greater the impact a particular increase in C, I, G, or Xn will have on the nation's GDP.

B. The Crowding-Out Effect. If government spending increases without an increase in taxes, the government must borrow money from the private sector to finance its deficit.

   1. The increase in demand from the government for funds in the private sector drives up the interest rates paid by firms for investment, and therefore decreases the quantity of private investment demand.

   2. "Crowding out" refers to the fall in private investment demand resulting from a government's deficit-financed expansionary fiscal policy. It can be illustrated in the Investment Demand diagram as follows:

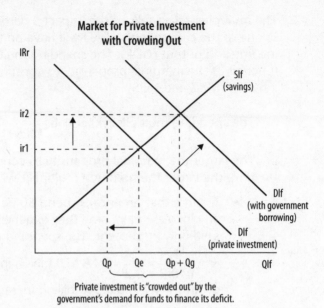

Market for Private Investment with Crowding Out

Private investment is "crowded out" by the government's demand for funds to finance its deficit.

i. In the graph above, the government demands funds from the private sector by selling bonds to pay for its budget deficit.

ii. The higher demand for funds in the economy drives up the interest rate paid by private firms for investment, reducing the quantity of private investment.

iii. While total spending increases to Qp + Qg, private investment falls from Qe to Qp, reducing the expansionary effect of the initial increase in government spending.

iv. Private sectors investment is thereby "crowded out" by government spending.

C. The multiplier effect and crowding-out effect are used to argue, respectively, for and against the use of expansionary fiscal policies to fight recessions.

1. The multiplier effect supports the view that an increase in government spending during a recession can have a significant impact on the level of aggregate demand and national output, effectively pushing an economy back toward its full employment level of output.

2. The crowding-out effect supports the opposing view that an increase in government spending and a decrease in taxes during a recession will have a weaker impact on aggregate demand, since the increase in AD caused by more G will be partially offset by a fall in I.

Test Tip

The crowding-out effect can be illustrated in the Investment Demand/Loanable Funds diagram in two ways. The graph here shows demand increasing and the higher interest rates leading to a fall in private investment. However, the AP would also accept a diagram showing supply decreasing, explained by the fact that as the government sells more bonds to finance its deficit, there is less savings in the private market for loanable funds, leading to a higher interest rate and less investment. Your teacher may teach you either method of illustrating crowding out, and either one is acceptable on the AP exam.

Aggregate Supply

Aggregate Supply—Short-Run Analysis

A. A nation's aggregate supply is the total amount of goods and services that all the firms in all the industries in a country will produce at every price level in a given period of time. The aggregate supply curve illustrates the relationship between the average price level in a nation and the total output of the nation's producers.

B. The Short-Run Aggregate Supply Curve/The Sticky-Wage and Price Model.

1. In the short run, the level of wages and other costs of production in a nation are relatively inflexible, meaning that workers will not accept lower wages when firms wish to reduce their costs. Therefore, firms find it difficult to lower their prices and instead must reduce output and layoff workers when aggregate demand falls in the nation. On the other hand, when prices of goods rise as aggregate demand shifts right, firms are able to take advantage of unchanging "sticky" wages and make more goods.

2. The short-run aggregate supply curve (SRAS) is upward sloping, but is

   i. Relatively flat below the full-employment level of output because of this wage stickiness.

   ii. Relatively steep beyond the full-employment level of output because there are physical constraints to what can be produced.

3. In the graph below, assume the nation is producing at the intersection of AD and AS, at the full-employment level of output of Y1.

The AD/AS Model: Short Run

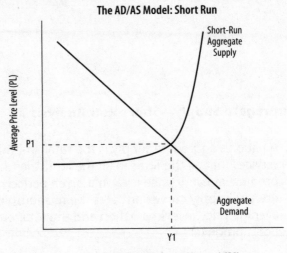

4. The nation's aggregate demand and aggregate supply intersect at Y1 and P1. This is the equilibrium level of national output. If AD falls (due to a fall in C, I, G, or Xn), there will be a new equilibrium level in the short run below Y1.

The AD/AS Model: Short Run

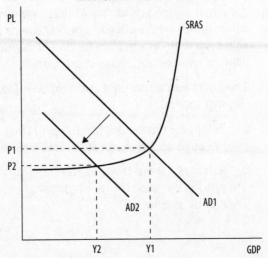

    i.   AD has fallen to AD2 (either due to a fall in C, I, G, or Xn). The new equilibrium level of output is Y2, and the price level is P2.

    ii. Due to the inflexibility of wages, firms have had to fire workers to cut their costs in response to falling demand. Producing a level of output equal to Y2 requires fewer workers than Y1, so unemployment rises in the short run.

C. The short-run aggregate supply curve (SRAS) is known as the sticky wage and price model of aggregate supply, since it shows the effect of a change in AD in an economy in which wages and input prices are slow to adjust to a change in the level of demand in a nation.

   1. Assume a nation producing at its full employment level of output experiences an increase in AD caused by a growth in C, I, G, or Xn. Since wages are inflexible in the short run, firms will demand more workers to meet the growing demand for their output. In the AD/AS model, output increases and the price level rises.

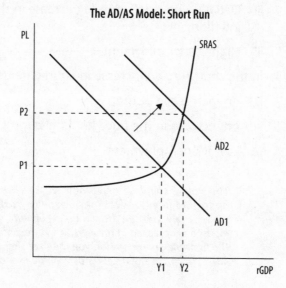

The AD/AS Model: Short Run

i. In the graph above, an increase in one of the components of AD has shifted AD to the right. Output grows beyond the full-employment level of Y1, but the price level rises by more.

ii. The graph above shows demand-pull inflation. In the short run, since wages are unlikely to rise, firms will hire more workers and increase their output to meet the rising demand.

iii. However, since the economy was already producing at full employment, output cannot grow by very much beyond Y1.

iv. Since labor and other resources have become scarcer and production has become less efficient and more costly as it is stretched toward its limit, the increase in demand causes a significant increase in the price level, as more demand is chasing the same amount of goods and services (this is demand-pull inflation).

2. In the short run, a fall in aggregate demand leads to:

i. A fall in output;

ii. Deflation or disinflation (a decrease in the rate of inflation);

iii. Higher unemployment.

3. In the short run, an increase in aggregate demand leads to:

i. An increase in output;

ii. An increase in the price level (inflation);

iii. Lower unemployment.

Test Tip

There are a couple of acceptable ways to draw the short-run aggregate supply curve. The bowed line used here is one way; alternatively, you can draw a simple upward sloping line. Either method is accepted in answers to free-response questions. In the multiple-choice section you may see simple upward sloping SRAS curves, or bowed lines as well. Be prepared for either.

II. Aggregate Supply—Long-Run Analysis

A. Long-run aggregate supply (LRAS) refers to the level of output of a nation's producers in response to a change in the price level in the period of time over which wages and other costs of production are flexible. The LRAS model is known, therefore, as the flexible wage model.

B. In the long run, workers will demand higher wages in response to an increase in aggregate demand and inflation, or be willing to accept lower wages in response to a decrease in aggregate demand, deflation, and rising unemployment.

C. In the long run, output will return to its full-employment level as wages and other prices adjust to the level of demand in the economy.

1. The LRAS curve is vertical at the full-employment level of output.

2. This illustrates the idea that once its labor market has settled into equilibrium, there is a quantity of goods a society will produce that is independent of the price level.

3. Note that this is quite different from the SRAS curve (and most other supply curves), which shows a positive slope to illustrate a direct relationship between price level and quantity of real output.

The AD/AS Model: Long-Run

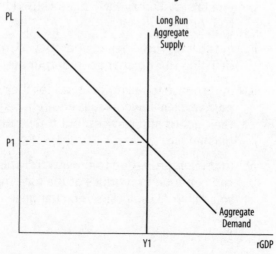

4. In the graph above, the AS curve is vertical at Y1, which corresponds with the nation's full-employment level of output.

   i. At Y1, the unemployment rate in the economy is equal to the NRU.

   ii. The nation is producing just inside its production possibilities curve.

5. Any change in AD in the graph above will have no effect on national output in the long run. Assume AD decreases:

The AD/AS Model: Long Run

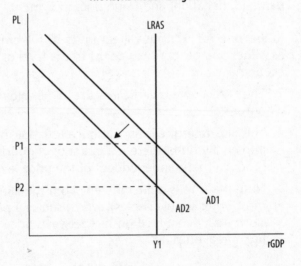

   i. The fall in AD may have been caused by a decrease in C, I, G, or Xn.

   ii. In the long run, a fall in aggregate demand will cause deflation but no change in output or employment.

   iii. In response to falling demand for their output, firms paid workers lower wages and reduced the prices of their goods and services, but total output remained unchanged.

   iv. In the long run, due to downwardly flexible wages, firms can continue to produce at the full-employment level, so a fall in AD will cause no change in output and employment but a decrease in the average price level and deflation.

6. An increase in AD causes no change in output and an increase in the price level in the long run, as in the following graph:

The AD/AS Model: Long Run

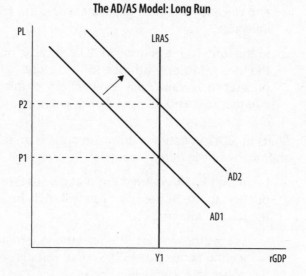

i. The increase in AD may have been caused by an increase in C, I, G, or Xn.

ii. In the long run, an increase in AD will cause inflation but no change in the level of output or employment.

iii. In response to the rising demand for the goods and services they produced, workers become increasingly scarce and demand higher wages, forcing firms to pay higher wages.

iv. In the long run, due to upwardly flexible wages, firms cannot afford to produce beyond the full-employment level, so an increase in AD will cause no change in output but an increase in the average price level and the inflation rate.

III. Determinants of Aggregate Supply

A. A change in the price level in a nation will lead to a movement along the nation's aggregate supply curve, as firms respond to the change in AD that causes the price level to change.

1. In the short run, a change in AD will cause output to change and price level to change, since wages are relatively sticky or inflexible.

2. In the long run, a change in AD will cause no change in the level of output, but due to the flexibility of wages and prices, the average price level will rise or fall depending on whether demand increased or decreased.

B. Shifts in SRAS. A nation's short-run aggregate supply curve will shift if any of the determinants of SRAS change.

1. Decreases in SRAS. Anything that causes firms' costs of production to rise in the short run will shift the SRAS curve to the left, including:

   i. Wages for workers. If wages rise due to any of the following factors, the SRAS curve will shift to the left and aggregate supply will decrease:

      ➤ Stronger labor unions;

      ➤ Higher minimum wage;

      ➤ Increased competition for labor;

      ➤ A decrease in the size of the labor force.

   ii. Business taxes. An increase in taxes paid by businesses to government will cause the SRAS curve to shift to the left.

   iii. Energy costs. An increase in energy costs, due to higher oil or gas prices, will reduce the level of SRAS, shifting the curve to the left. A rise in the cost of any common input product would have this same effect.

   iv. Rents and interest. An increase in rental rates or interest rates will raise firms' costs for land and capital, respectively, and shift the SRAS curve to the left.

2. An increase in costs of production in a nation is known as a negative supply shock, which causes the SRAS curve to shift to the left, increasing the equilibrium price level and reducing the equilibrium level of output, as seen below:

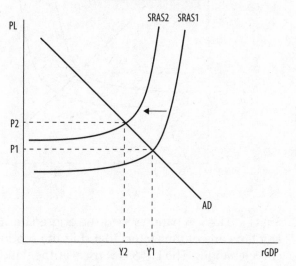

The AD/AS Model: Short Run

3. Increases in SRAS. Anything that causes the costs of production faced by a nation's firms to decrease will cause the SRAS curve to increase and shift to the right, including:

   i.   Lower wages for workers;

   ii. Lower business taxes;

   iii. Lower energy costs;

   iv. Lower rents and interest rates.

4. A decrease in costs of production in a nation is known as a positive supply shock, which shifts SRAS to the right, causing the level of output to increase and the average price level to decrease, as seen below:

The AD/AS Model: Short Run

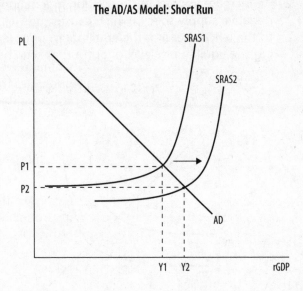

C. Shifts in LRAS. A nation's long-run aggregate supply curve shifts any time any of the factors that shift the production possibilities curve changes. The LRAS is vertical at the nation's full-employment level of real GDP; therefore, when LRAS shifts, the level of output the nation is capable of changes. Factors that may shift the LRAS curve include:

1. An increase in the quantity of the factors of production, including:

   i.   A larger workforce, which may result from population growth, immigration, or people voluntarily entering the workforce.

   ii. An increase in land resources, which may result from new discoveries of minerals or raw materials, territorial expansion, or military conquest.

   iii. An increase in capital stock, which will result from investments in technology by the private or public sector.

2. An increase in the quality of the factors of production, including:

i.   A better educated and more highly skilled workforce, which will result from more investment in schools and job training facilities, also known as human capital.

ii. An improvement in the quality of land resources, resulting from better extraction technologies for raw materials, fertilizers and chemical pesticides that increase agricultural yields, or an improvement in techniques for harvesting forest and marine resources.

iii. An improvement in capital, which may result from technological innovation.

3. A nation's LRAS curve will increase, along with its full-employment level of output, and its production possibilities curve, when any of the above determinants of LRAS change.

The AD/AS Model: Long Run

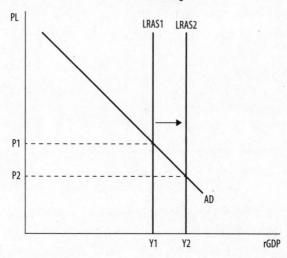

4. Decreases in LRAS are more rare but could result from any of the following:

i.   A decrease in the size of the population or the size of the workforce;

ii. The depletion of land resources or a loss of land in a territorial dispute or war;

    iii. The destruction of capital due to war or natural disaster;

    iv. A deterioration of the nation's infrastructure or education system over a period of time.

5. Any of the above can reduce the level of full-employment output in a nation over time and shift the LRAS and the PPC to the left. Such factors will lead to a deterioration in the standards of living of the nation's people and are thus considered very undesirable events.

Test Tip

Be familiar with the various determinants of aggregate supply. You should also know whether a change in a certain factor (such as business taxes, oil prices, or labor productivity) affects SRAS, LRAS, or both.

Macroeconomic Equilibrium in the AD/AS Model

Real Output and Price Level in the AD/AS Model

A. Short-Run Equilibrium in the AD/AS Model. At any point in time, a nation's short-run equilibrium level of income and the average price level are illustrated in the AD/AS model as the intersection of aggregate demand and short-run aggregate supply, as seen below:

Equilibrium in the AD/AS Model

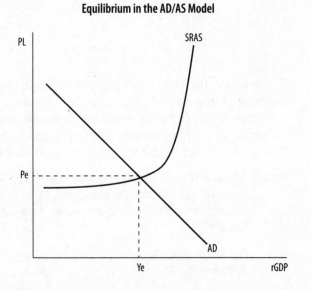

1. In the graph above, the nation's equilibrium price level is Pe and its equilibrium level of output is Ye.

2. Equilibrium output can be compared to full-employment (or long- run equilibrium) output by including a long-run aggregate supply curve in the diagram above.

Recessionary Gap in the AD/AS Model

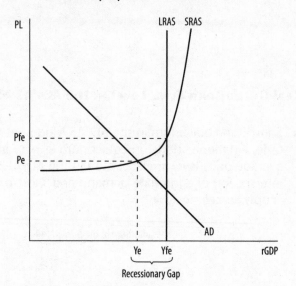

3. We know that LRAS intersects the horizontal axis at the full-employment level of output, so we can conclude that if the nation were producing at full employment, it would be producing at a higher level of output (Yfe) and a higher average price level (Pfe) than it is in its current equilibrium (Ye and Pe).

i.   The country in the figure above is currently in equilibrium below the full-employment level of output. The country is experiencing a recessionary gap equal to Yfe – Ye.

ii. A recessionary gap could be caused by any of the following:

> A decrease in households' consumption patterns;

> A decrease in private investment by firms;

> A decrease in government spending (or an increase in taxes);

> A decrease in net exports.

4. Short-run equilibrium may also occur at the full-employment level of output. If a nation is achieving its macroeconomic objectives of full employment and price stability, then the AD and SRAS curves intersect at the LRAS curve, as seen below:

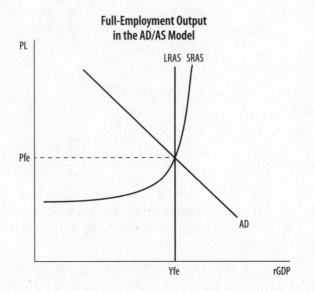

Full-Employment Output in the AD/AS Model

5. The country above is achieving its macroeconomic objectives:

   i. It is producing at its full-employment level of output;

   ii. It has a stable rate of inflation; and

   iii. The unemployment rate is equal to the natural rate of unemployment or NRU (see Chapter 7), which means there is structural and frictional unemployment, but there is no cyclical unemployment.

   iv. Short- and long-run equilibrium are the same in this case, with a price level of Pfe and a level of real output of Yfe.

6. A country can also be producing at a short-run equilibrium level that is *beyond* the full-employment level of output, as seen below:

Inflationary Gap in the AD/AS Model

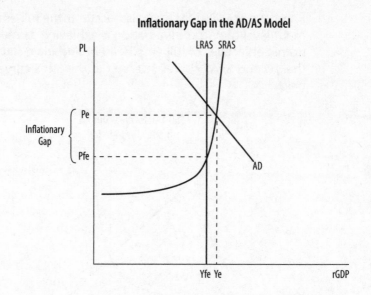

7. A nation will produce beyond its full-employment level of output in the short run if any of the following changes occur:

   i.   An increase in household consumption;

   ii. An increase in private investment in capital by firms;

   iii. An increase in government spending or a decrease in taxes;

   iv. An increase in net exports.

8. It is possible to produce beyond full employment in the short run because there is some unemployment of labor and other resources even when an economy is at full employment.

   i.   Since wages are inflexible in the short run, firms will find it profitable to hire more workers at the same wage rate to meet the rising demand for their output.

   ii. Since SRAS is highly unresponsive to changes in demand beyond full employment, the increase in the price level will be proportionally larger than the increase in output beyond Yfe.

  iii. The level of output beyond full-employment level is typically not sustainable over periods of time. Much like a sprinter or other athlete engaged in anaerobic exercise, this situation places heavy demands on productive resources and cannot continue indefinitely.

II. From Short Run to Long Run in the AD/AS Model

A. In the long run, a nation will always produce at its full-employment level of output, regardless of the level of aggregate demand. This means that long-run equilibrium will always be found where AD intersects LRAS on the graph.

B. In the long run, wages and prices are perfectly flexible and will adjust to the level of demand for the nation's goods and services.

 1. Following a decrease in AD, in the short run,

  i. Output will fall due to the fact that firms must reduce labor to cut costs and remain competitive.

  ii. Price level will fall, but only slightly, because since firms cannot cut wages, they cannot reduce their prices by very much.

  iii. Unemployment will increase as firms reduce their workforces to cut costs and remain competitive.

 2. Following a decrease in AD, in the long run,

  i. SRAS shifts to the right, because the high unemployment resulting from firms laying off workers in the short run causes the wage rate to fall because workers who are unemployed for periods of time are often willing to work at lower wages.

  ii. The intersection of the new lower AD and the new SRAS will occur at the full-employment level once wages have fallen and SRAS has shifted down and to the right.

iii. Output returns to the full-employment level because the lower prices achievable at the lower wage rate increase the quantity of national output demanded over time.

iv. Unemployment returns to the natural rate of unemployment, meaning only those who are structurally and frictionally unemployed are unable to find jobs at the prevailing wage rates.

v. Workers' nominal wages are lower, since they were willing to accept lower wages rather than remaining unemployed. Real wages, however, are at the same level they were before the fall in AD since the average price level is now lower than before AD fell in the first place.

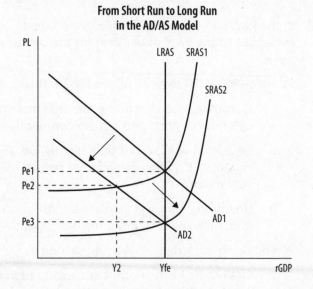

**From Short Run to Long Run
in the AD/AS Model**

vi. In the graph above, a fall in AD causes output to fall in the short run to Y2 and price level to fall to Pe2. As people adjust to this new lower price level, we transition to the long run. In the long run, high unemployment causes wages to fall, shifting SRAS rightward and increasing output back to Yfe. The full-employment price level following the decrease in the wage rate is Pe3, but output has returned to Yfe.

vii. Macroeconomists disagree widely about the degree to which wages are downwardly flexible. Classical or neoclassical economists, who borrow their ideas from Adam Smith's laissez-faire beliefs, tend to think this self-correction works better than Keynesian economists do. Economists that borrow their ideas from John Meynard Keynes tend to think that expansionary governmental policy is needed to shift AD to the right because SRAS will not shift right on its own.

3. Following an increase in AD in the short run,

   i. Output will increase due to the higher demand for the nation's goods and services;

   ii. The price level will rise due to there being more demand but no change in aggregate supply;

   iii. Unemployment will fall as firms hire more workers at the same wage rate to meet rising demand.

4. Following an increase in AD in the long run,

   i. SRAS will shift to the left because the unemployment rate falls below the natural rate when AD rises, increasing the scarcity of labor and forcing firms to compete for workers, driving up the wage rate;

   ii. The intersection of the higher AD curve and the new SRAS curve will occur at the full-employment level once wages have adjusted and SRAS has shifted to the left;

   iii. Output will return to the full-employment level because the higher prices necessitated by the higher wage rate will reduce the quantity of national output demanded over time;

   iv. Unemployment will increase once again to the natural rate, meaning only those who are structurally and frictionally unemployed will be without work at the prevailing wage rates;

   v. Workers' nominal wages are higher, since the shortage of labor drove up the wage rate, but their real wages are the same as they were before the increase in AD since the average price level is higher.

From Short Run to Long Run in the AD/AS Model

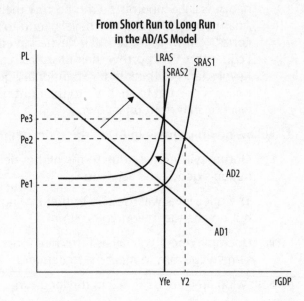

vi. In the graph above, an increase in AD causes prices to rise, and labor to become scarcer as more workers are needed to generate the new Y2 level of output than the Yfe level. In the long run, workers demand higher wages, which shifts SRAS left and returns the equilibrium level of output to the full employment level. The average price level has risen and inflation is now higher than it was before the increase in AD.

Many questions on the multiple-choice section will ask you to determine how certain changes in AD and AS will affect employment, prices levels, output, and so on. Practice shifting the curves and determine how different macroeconomic indicators are affected to prepare for these types of questions.

III. Economic Fluctuations in the AD/AS Model

A. Any change in aggregate demand or aggregate supply causes a change in the short-run equilibrium level of output and the average price level in a nation.

B. An economy may experience a variety of "shocks," both positive and negative, to both aggregate demand and aggregate supply, that will impact the level of real output and prices.

C. Negative Demand Shocks. A negative demand shock is anything that causes a sudden, unexpected fall in consumption, investment, or net exports, thereby reducing the total of demand for a nation's output.

1. Negative demand shocks could result from:

    i. A collapse in house prices. Houses are an important asset and source of wealth to a nation's consumers. A fall in house prices will reduce wealth, which is a determinant of consumption. As consumption falls, AD will fall.

    ii. A fall in the value of stocks. Like houses, stocks are a source of a household's wealth, and a fall in the stock market will cause consumers to spend less and AD to fall.

    iii. A tightening of credit markets. Credit markets consist of the financial institutions that make loans available to firms and households for financing investment. When bank confidence is low, firms find it hard to borrow to acquire new capital or finance their payrolls, investment falls, and AD shifts to the left.

    iv. A fall in foreign incomes. If a trading nation enters a recession, demand for the home nation's goods and services will fall abroad, reducing net exports and shifting AD to the left.

2. A negative demand shock will cause output to fall in the short run, unemployment to rise, and put downward pres-

sure on the price level. In the long run, if demand does not recover on its own or through government intervention, the nation will return to full-employment output at a lower price level, as seen below:

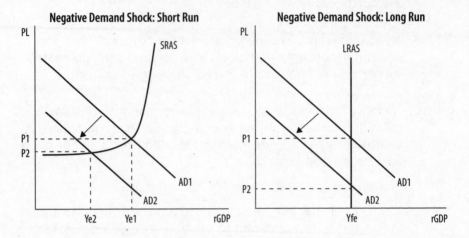

Negative Demand Shock: Short Run

Negative Demand Shock: Long Run

D. Positive Demand Shocks. A positive demand shock results from anything that causes a sudden, unexpected increase in consumption, investment, or net exports, thereby increasing the total demand for a nation's output.

1. Positive demand shocks may result from:

    i. A rapid increase in house or stock prices;

    ii. The development of a new technology that spurs new investment by firms, such as the Internet or mobile computing;

    iii. Financial innovation that increases the availability of credit to households and firms, allowing them to easily acquire finances for consumption and investment;

    iv. Rising incomes abroad, which will lead to an increase in net exports and a boost to AD.

2. A positive demand shock will shift the AD curve to the right, creating short-run economic growth and a fall in unem-

ployment. If AD remains strong and there are no efforts by government to bring inflation under control, in the long run the economy will return to its full-employment level with a higher rate of inflation, as seen below.

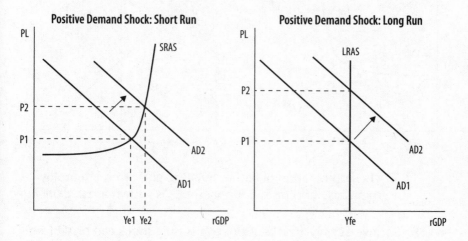

E. Negative Supply Shocks. Anything that causes a sudden, unexpected increase in the costs of production to firms will cause a negative supply shock, reducing the level of output possible in a nation, increasing the price level, and increasing the unemployment rate.

1. Negative supply shocks could result from:

i. Higher energy costs;

ii. Higher minimum wage;

iii. Higher taxes on firms.

2. Negative supply shocks will cause SRAS to shift inward, to the left, driving up the price level and unemployment, reducing the level of output in the economy. In the long run, the rising unemployment will put downward pressure on wages, and any increase in costs that caused the supply shock will in theory be offset by lower labor costs, moving the economy back to its full-employment level and reducing inflation.

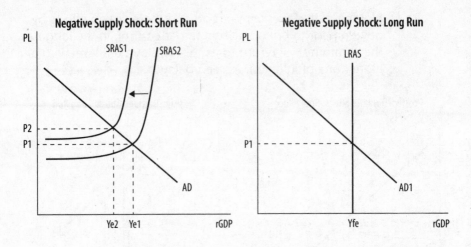

3. The combination of higher inflation and rising unemployment resulting from a supply shock is known as *stagflation*.

F. Positive Supply Shocks. A positive supply shock can result from anything that leads to a sudden increase in productivity of the nation's resources or a reduction in costs of production for firms, which shifts SRAS (and in some cases LRAS) to the right, increasing the full-employment level of output and reducing the level of inflation in the economy.

1. Positive supply shocks could result from:

   i. Lower business taxes;

   ii. Reduction or elimination of the minimum wage;

   iii. A reduction in trade union power;

   iv. New productivity-enhancing technology;

   v. Discovery of a new productive resource;

   vi. An inflow of foreign investment in capital;

   vii. An inflow of skilled workers willing to work for lower wages;

viii. Better education and training for workers (human capital) or other increases in the capital stock.

2. A positive supply shock will cause both SRAS and LRAS to
shift to the right, increasing the nation's full-employment
level of output, putting downward pressure on the price level, and possibly reducing the natural rate of unemployment.

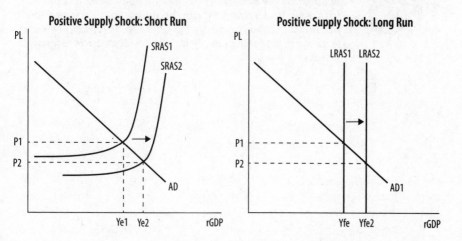

3. A positive supply shock in the AD/AS model corresponds
with the accomplishment of the three macroeconomic
objectives, and is therefore the most desired outcome of any
country.

   i.   Economic Growth. The full-employment level of output
        increases with an increase in aggregate supply, mean-
        ing the nation is capable of producing a greater level
        of output when using its resources to their fullest
        potential.

   ii. Low Unemployment. As output grows from Yfe to Yfe2,
        unemployment falls, assuring that a greater percentage
        of the country's labor force is able to find work.

   iii. Price-Level Stability. The downward pressure on the average price level resulting from an increase in AS allows growth to occur without inflation.

Understanding the difference between how a change in aggregate demand affects an economy in the short run and in the long run is important, as this is commonly tested in both the multiple-choice and free-response questions. You must be able to explain that in the long run, because wages and prices are flexible, an economy will always return to its full employment level of output following any increase or decrease in aggregate demand.

PART V

FINANCIAL SECTOR

Money, Banking, and Financial Markets

I. **The Definitions of Financial Assets: Stocks, Bonds, and Money**

A. Stocks. A *stock* is a share in the ownership of a business which can be bought or sold by investors who wish to hold ownership rights of publicly traded companies.

1. A *shareholder* is an individual or institution that holds stock in another company.

2. Shareholders are granted special privileges as part owners of a company, including:

   i. The right to vote in elections for new members of the company's board of directors;

   ii. The right to share in distributions (dividends) of the company's profit;

   iii. The right to purchase new shares issued by the company;

   iv. The right to a company's assets during a liquidation of the company.

3. Stocks are a relatively non-liquid asset, meaning that they cannot be used as a medium of exchange in transactions in a product or resource market. A stock can be sold on a stock market for money, which is a liquid asset, meaning it can be spent on goods, services, or resources.

B. Bonds. A *bond* is a certificate of debt issued by a company or a government to an investor. The bond issuer is obliged to pay the bond holder a debt as well as an interest payment. The purchaser of a bond (the creditor) makes a loan to the issuer of the bond (the debtor) in exchange for an interest payment and a promise to repay the principal at a future date.

1. Bonds differ from stocks in that the owner of a stock is an equity owner of the company, meaning he or she partially owns the company whose stock is purchased. In contrast, a bond holder is a creditor to the company or government whose bond is purchased, meaning the issuer is in debt to the bond holder. Stocks are thus assets that come with more upside and downside risk than bonds.

2. Government bonds are issued to allow governments to finance current expenditures without having to raise tax revenues to do so. They allow a government to deficit spend.

3. Company-issued bonds (sometimes called "commercial paper") allow for the financing of long-term investments by firms.

4. Typically, company bonds are considered more risky investments than government bonds, and thus offer a higher interest rate to compensate for the increased risk to lenders.

5. The higher the risk that the issuer of a particular bond will not repay the principal, the higher the interest rate lenders will demand.

C. Money. *Money* is any object that can be used in payment for goods and services.

1. Money has three primary functions:

    i.   Money is a store of value. It can be held onto today to be used in the future for exchanges in a market. Things that do not retain value well are not very useful as money.

    ii. Money is a unit of account. Money can be used to state the value of something in terms of one type of money (currency) or another. For example, a haircut costs $15. This is an account of the value of a haircut. Speaking this way helps people easily compare quantities of different goods.

iii. Money is a medium of exchange. Money helps facilitate the easy exchange of goods and services between buyers and sellers in markets. Without money, goods and services would have to be bartered for one another, requiring a double coincidence of wants. In an economy with money, trades are easier to arrange and more people benefit from those trades.

2. Money differs from stocks and bonds because of its liquidity, or the ability to use it easily as a medium of exchange. Stocks and bonds are less liquid stores of value, because they must first be sold, or "liquidated," in order to be converted to money and spent on goods or services. Other assets that people use to hold wealth, such as gold or land, can be even less liquid (even more difficult to convert into a readily spendable form).

3. Money may take several forms, from more liquid forms to less liquid forms.

i. M1. This includes the money in an economy held as coins, cash, and checking-account deposits. M1 is the most liquid form and narrowest measure of money.

ii. M2. This includes M1 plus savings accounts and small time deposits (accounts held at banks that cannot be drawn from within a certain period of time, which allows the bank to invest the funds in less liquid assets). The M2 measure of money is broader than M1 and slightly less liquid.

iii. M3. This includes M1 plus M2 plus larger time deposits, and thus is a more illiquid form of money than M2.

iv. Broader measures of money, such as MZM (money zero maturity), are more inclusive of "near monies" and even less liquid than M3.

II. The Money Supply

A. A nation's money supply refers to the amount of money available to households and firms at any particular time. It measures the total amount in a nation held as cash, coins, and checkable deposits (checking accounts).

B. The supply of money in the economy has a major impact on several macroeconomic indicators, including rates of interest, private investment, and inflation.

C. The money supply is determined primarily by a country's central bank, known as the Federal Reserve Bank in the United States. The "Fed" attempts to influence interest rates through policies aimed at increasing or decreasing the supply of money in the United States, which can be represented by the money supply curve.

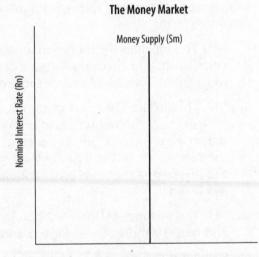

The Money Market

Money Supply (Sm)

Nominal Interest Rate (Rn)

Quantity of Money (Qm)

1. In the money market diagram above, the supply of money is vertical, or perfectly inelastic, because it is determined by the monetary policy actions of the central bank and is independent of the nominal interest rate.

2. The "price of money" is the nominal interest rate, which reflects the opportunity cost of spending money (what would be given up by not saving) or the cost of borrowing money (what must be paid in addition to the amount borrowed).

3. The money supply refers to the *liquid* forms of money including the amount in currency and in checking accounts at commercial banks.

III. Banks and the Creation of Money

A. A nation's commercial (for profit) banks are generally regulated by the central bank (the Fed in the United States). The primary activities of commercial banks are:

1. Accepting checking and savings deposits from the community, on which the bank pays a particular rate of interest.

    i. Funds deposited in a bank are assets for the depositor (since the depositor is owed the amount deposited plus interest).

    ii. Funds deposited in a bank are liabilities for the bank (since the bank owes the amount deposited plus interest).

2. Making loans to borrowers, both households and firms, on which the borrowers pay the bank a particular rate of interest.

    i. A loan is an asset to the bank (since the bank is owed the amount loaned plus interest).

    ii. A loan is a liability to the borrower (since he or she owes the amount borrowed plus interest to the bank).

3. A commercial bank's profits come from the difference between the interest rate charged on its assets (the loans it makes to borrowers) minus the interest rate it pays on its liabilities (the deposits from the community).

B. Required Reserves. A commercial bank is required by the central bank to keep a particular percentage of its total deposits from the community "on reserve," meaning it cannot loan out 100 percent of the money deposited by the community.

1. Required reserves allow depositors the ability to withdraw funds from their checking accounts on a daily basis.

2. In the United States, commercial banks' required reserves are primarily stored at the regional Federal Reserve Bank.

3. The percentage of total deposits banks are required to keep on reserve depends on the required reserve ratio, which itself is determined by the Federal Reserve Bank.

C. The Required Reserve Ratio (RRR). The RRR is the percentage of total deposits that a commercial bank must keep in reserve in order to meet the demands of its depositors for money from day-to-day.

1. It is expressed as a decimal. For instance:

   i.   A RRR of 0.2 would require banks to keep $0.20 of every $1 in total deposits on reserve, allowing the bank to loan out the other $0.80 of every dollar of its liabilities.

   ii. A RRR of 0.1 would allow banks to loan out and earn interest on 90 percent of their total deposits, keeping only 10 percent on reserve.

   iii. The Fed pays only a very low interest rate to commercial banks on their reserves, while excess reserves loaned to customers earn higher rates of interest for commercial banks.

   iv. Since commercial banks earn almost no interest on their reserves kept at the Fed, banks generally prefer to be able to loan out a greater proportion of their total deposits.

2. Excess Reserves. Any amount held in reserve by a commercial bank beyond what is required by the Fed is known as excess reserves.

   i.   When excess reserves in the banking system increase, the money supply curve shifts to the right.

ii. When excess reserves decrease, the money supply curve shifts to the left.

iii. The level of excess reserves in the banking system depends primarily on the monetary policies of the Federal Reserve Bank.

> ➤ Increasing the RRR reduces the amount of excess reserves and reduces the money supply.

> ➤ Reducing the RRR increases the amount of excess reserves and increases the money supply.

Test Tip

It is important to read multiple-choice questions very carefully before moving on to the answers. For example, the following question can be misinterpreted if not read carefully. Assume the required reserve ratio is 20% and a bank receives a new deposit of $1,000. How much does the bank's required reserves increase by? *A similar question may conclude with* How much does the bank's excess reserves increase by? *While only one word has changed in the question, the answer is clearly going to be very different. Read carefully to determine exactly what a question is asking for.*

D. The Creation of Money by Commercial Banks

1. When a household makes a deposit to a commercial bank, the bank will wish to loan out most of these deposited funds, since it is through lending money that commercial banks earn profits (charging a higher rate of interest to borrowers than they pay to depositors).

2. Assume a RRR of 0.2. When a deposit of $100 is made, the bank will loan out $80 of it and keep $20 on reserve, as required by the Fed. The bank's loaning out of $80, however, creates new money in the economy, since the borrower of the $80 now holds currency that he or she would not have had access to without the bank acting as an intermediary between depositors and borrowers.

3. The creation of money by commercial banks continues through the multiple expansion of checkable deposits (i.e., the bank's ability to loan out one person's savings to another person, who is able to spend the money in the economy).

The RRR is 0.2. A deposit of $100 into one bank will lead to an
increase in checkable deposits across the banking system as follows:

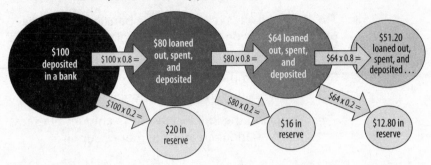

4. In the fashion depicted above, any change in checkable deposits in the commercial banking system will lead to multiple expansions of checkable deposits throughout the system.

5. A bank will typically want to loan out as high a percentage of its deposits as is allowed by the Fed, which creates new spending and new deposits in other banks, which themselves will make new loans, further expanding the supply of money in the banking system.

E. The Money Multiplier. The ultimate amount by which an increase in checkable deposits in the banking system is capable of increasing the total money supply depends on the money multiplier (m).

1. The money multiplier (m) equals one divided by the required reserve ratio (RRR): $m = \dfrac{1}{\text{RRR}}$.

2. For instance, assume the Fed requires banks to keep 20 percent of their total deposits on reserve. The RRR = 0.2.

   i. $m = \dfrac{1}{0.2} = 5$.

   ii. An increase in checkable deposits will ultimately increase the supply of money in the banking system by as much as five times the initial deposit, assuming the deposit was not already part of the money supply.

iii. If banks' reserves increase because of actions by the Federal Reserve, such as the purchase of government bonds from commercial banks by the Fed, then the money deposited would not have been part of the money supply to begin with, so the increase in the money supply will include the initial change in deposits. For example:

➤ Assume the Fed buys $100 billion worth of government bonds from the commercial banks, and the RRR = 0.2.

➤ The money supply will increase by a multiple of $100 billion, specifically by five times the initial change in deposits, so the money supply grows by up to $500 billion (= $100 billion × 5).

iv. If a household deposits $100 previously held as cash into a checking account, the supply of checkable deposits will increase by as much as $100 × 5 = $500. The money supply, on the other hand, can only grow by a maximum $400, since the initial $100 deposit was already part of the money supply.

v. In practice, two factors weaken the degree to which deposits and bond purchases cause the money supply to expand:

➤ If the public holds some money in cash rather than depositing it into banks, then the process is weakened because banks don't re-lend as much money at each step in the process.

➤ If commercial banks hold more reserves than the Fed requires them to, then the process is weakened because less is lent at each step of the process.

Test Tip

Practice using the required reserve ratio and the money multiplier to calculate the effects of changes in checkable deposits in the banking system on required reserves, excess reserves, and the total reserves in the banking system. Typically there will be four or five multiple-choice questions phrased in various ways requiring the use of the RRR and the money multiplier.

IV. Money Demand

A. There are two reasons money is demanded in an economy: as an asset used to preserve wealth in a liquid form for the future or to use in transactions in the product or resource markets.

B. Asset Demand. Money is an asset itself, in that it is a store of value for future use. Money held as an asset can be kept by households or firms to acquire goods, services, or resources at some time in the future.

1. The asset demand for money is inversely related to the interest rate in the economy.

    i.   The higher the interest rate, the less quantity of money will be demanded as an asset, since the opportunity cost of holding on to money is greater.

    ii. At lower interest rates, households and firms will demand more money as an asset, since the opportunity cost of holding money is less when there is less interest to be earned by holding wealth in less liquid assets such as savings accounts, time deposits, and bonds.

    iii. The asset demand curve for money is downward sloping.

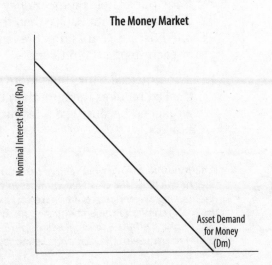

The Money Market

Nominal Interest Rate (Rn)

Asset Demand
for Money
(Dm)

Quantity of Money (Qm)

C. The transaction demand for money (M) refers to demand for liquidity with which to engage in the purchase of goods and services produced in the economy.

1. *M* depends on the level of output in the economy (Y), the velocity of money (V), and the average price level in the economy (P).

2. The monetary equation of exchange tells us the quantity of money demanded for transactions (M) based on these three variables: MV = PY.

    i. The greater the level of real output (Y) in an economy, the more money is needed to buy the output.

    ii. The less the level of output, the less money is demanded for transactions.

    iii. Other variables affecting transaction demand include the velocity of money (V), which measures the average number of times a dollar is spent in a year, and the price level (P).

3. At any given time, it is assumed that V and P are stable, so to simplify, we can say that the transaction demand for money is dependent only on the level of output in an economy, and is thus vertical at the level of national income.

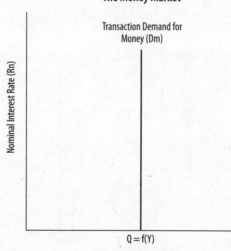

The Money Market

Transaction Demand for Money (Dm)

Nominal Interest Rate (Rn)

Q = f(Y)

Quantity of Money (Qm)

   i.   In the graph above, the quantity of money demanded for transactions (M) is a function of the nominal GDP (Y).

D. The Total Demand for Money. When we combine the downward sloping asset demand curve and the vertical transaction demand curve, the result is a downward sloping money demand (Dm) curve inversely related to the nominal interest rate (IRn) and dependent upon the level of national output and income (Y).

   1.   If Y increases, Dm shifts to the right.

   2.   If Y decreases, Dm shifts left.

V. The Money Market

A. The money market combines the supply of money and the demand for money in a nation's economy.

   1.   Money supply (Sm) is determined by the efforts of the central bank (the Fed) and includes all the money held as currency or as checkable deposits in a nation. Sm is vertical and unresponsive to changes in the interest rate.

   2.   Money demand (Dm) is the sum of the asset and transaction demand for money in a nation, and is inversely related to the interest rate.

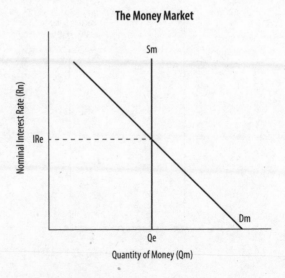

The Money Market

3. The equilibrium nominal interest rate in a nation is found at the intersection of Sm and Dm.

B. Changes in the Nominal Interest Rate. Anything that changes the supply of or the demand for money will lead to a change in the nominal interest rate. For instance:

1. An increase in the nominal GDP (Y) will lead to an increase in the transaction demand for money and shift Dm to the right.

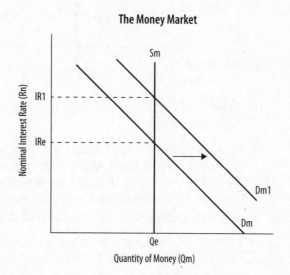

The Money Market

i. The increase in output will cause an increase in the demand for money for transactions.

ii. Assuming there is no change in the supply of money from the central bank, this will drive up interest rates, since banks can charge a greater fee for the privilege of borrowing and are willing to offer a greater rate to depositors for the privilege of accepting their deposits.

2. A fall in national output (Y) will lead to a decrease in the demand for money.

The Money Market

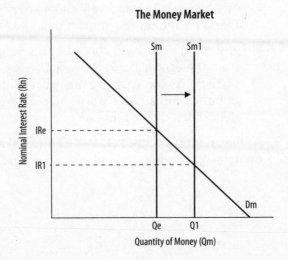

i. The fall in output causes a fall in the demand for money for transactions.

ii. Assuming there is no change in the supply of money from the central bank, this will drive down interest rates as banks are willing to make loans to the now scarce borrowers at a lower rate and willing to offer depositors a lower rate for their less-demanded deposits.

3. An increase in the supply of money due to a change in monetary policy by the central bank will lead to a decrease in the nominal interest rate.

The Money Market

    i.   A central bank policy expands the supply of excess reserves in commercial banks, typically by purchasing government bonds from those banks.

   ii.   The funds the central bank paid for the bonds are now excess reserves for the bank and can be lent out to create money.

  iii.   Money is less scarce, so banks are willing to make loans at a lower interest rate and pay lower returns to depositors.

4. A decrease in the money supply due to a change in monetary policy by the central bank will lead to an increase in the nominal interest rate:

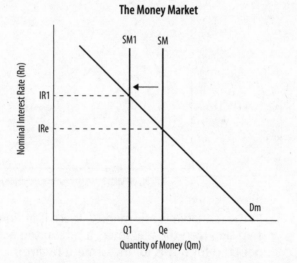

The Money Market

    i.   A central bank policy reduces the excess reserves in the banking system, typically by selling government bonds to commercial banks.

   ii.   The increased scarcity of money leads banks to charge a higher rate to borrowers and reward depositors with a higher nominal interest rate on their deposits.

VI. The Loanable Funds Market and Real Interest Rates

A. Investment demand is inversely related to the real interest rate in the economy. Real interest rates depend on

1. The nominal interest rate, and

2. Expectations about the inflation rate.

B. The demand for investment is illustrated in the market for loanable funds.

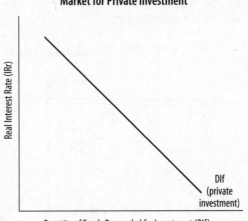

Market for Private Investment

Real Interest Rate (IRr)

DIf (private investment)

Quantity of Funds Demanded for Investment (QIf)

1. In the loanable funds market, there is an inverse relationship between the real interest rate in the economy and the demand for funds for investment by firms.

   i. At higher interest rates firms find fewer investment projects profitable and demand fewer funds for investment.

   ii. At lower interest rates firms find more investment projects profitable and demand more funds for investment.

2. The real interest rate is directly related to the nominal interest rate.

   i. Anything that increases nominal interest rates in the money market will drive up the real interest rate, assuming inflation does not change.

ii. Anything that decreases nominal interest rates will reduce the real rate of interest, assuming inflation does not change.

C. Changes in the nominal interest rate lead to changes in the level of private investment.

1. A policy that reduces the supply of money and increases the nominal interest rate will put upward pressure on real interest rates and reduce the quantity of funds demanded for investment by firms.

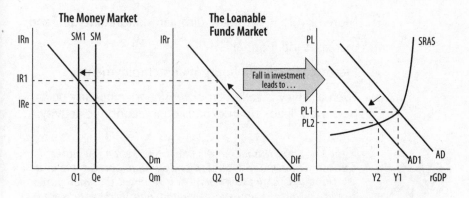

i. Less private investment reduces aggregate demand;

ii. Puts downward pressure on the average price level; and

iii. Reduces national output and employment.

iv. Such a policy is called a *contractionary monetary policy* because it leads to a contraction in economic activity.

2. A policy that increases the supply of money and decreases the nominal interest rate will put downward pressure on real interest rates and increase the quantity of funds demanded for investment.

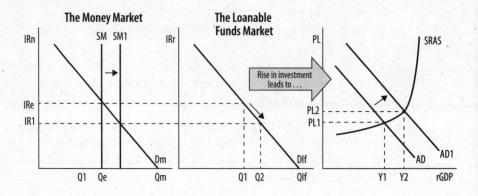

i. More private investment stimulates aggregate demand;

ii. Increases inflation; and

iii. Increases the level of output and employment.

iv. Such a policy is called an *expansionary monetary policy* because it leads to an expansion in economic activity.

The impact of changes in the money market on the market for investment demand/loanable funds is an important one as it is through changes to the level of investment that monetary policy affects the aggregate demand, and thereby the price level, the level of employment, and output.

Central Bank and Control of the Money Supply

I. Tools of Central Bank Policy

Central banks have three primary tools at their disposal to alter the money supply: adjustment of the reserve ratio, changes in the discount rate, and open-bond market operations used to influence the federal funds rate.

A. The Required Reserve Ratio (RRR). The RRR is the percentage of a commercial bank's total deposits that it must keep on reserve at any particular time.

1. Changing the RRR is a powerful tool of monetary policy available to the central bank, for two reasons:

    i.   It directly affects the quantity of excess reserves in the banking system.

    ii. It changes the size of the money multiplier, which impacts the money-creating ability of the private banking system.

    iii. Because of the extreme power of this tool, it is very infrequently used as a tool of monetary policy.

2. Impact on Excess Reserves. When the central bank (the "Fed" in the United States) changes the RRR, banks immediately find they either have more excess reserves than before (if the RRR is lowered) or must top up their reserves to meet the new higher requirement (if the RRR is increased).

    i.   Expansionary Monetary Policy. If the Fed wishes to increase the money supply, it can reduce the RRR.

➤ Commercial banks are now required to keep a smaller percentage of their total deposits on reserve.

➤ Their excess reserves increase, which means they are allowed to loan out more money than before.

➤ The money supply increases, and the nominal interest rate banks charge borrowers decreases.

ii. Contractionary Monetary Policy. If the Fed wishes to decrease the money supply, it can increase the RRR.

➤ Commercial banks are now required to keep a greater percentage of their total deposits on reserve.

➤ They must reduce the number of loans they make and top up their reserves at the Fed.

➤ The money supply decreases, and the nominal interest rates banks charge borrowers increases.

3. Impact on the Money Multiplier (m). Besides the immediate impact on the money supply, changing the reserve ratio also changes the size of the money multiplier, and thereby impacts the money-creating ability of the entire banking system.

i. Expansionary Monetary Policy. If the Fed reduces the RRR, the money multiplier (m) increases.

➤ Assume the RRR falls from 0.2 to 0.1.

➤ Before the change in the RRR, $m = \dfrac{1}{0.2} = 5$.

➤ After the change in the RRR, $m = \dfrac{1}{0.1} = 10$. Following the decrease in the RRR, the money multiplier increased from 5 to 10.

➤ For every dollar of new deposits in the banking system, up to $9 of new loans can be created, while before only $4 could have been created.

➤ Impact of a decrease in the RRR (expansionary monetary policy):

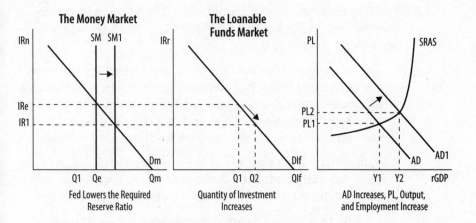

The Money Market   **The Loanable Funds Market**

Fed Lowers the Required Reserve Ratio

Quantity of Investment Increases

AD Increases, PL, Output, and Employment Increase

    ii.   Contractionary monetary policy. If the Fed increases the RRR, *m* decreases.

➤ Assume the RRR increases from 0.1 to 0.2.

➤ Now *m* decreases from 10 to 5.

➤ The money-creating ability of banks is diminished at a higher RRR, reducing the money supply and putting additional upward pressure on interest rates.

➤ Impact of an increase in the RRR (contractionary monetary policy):

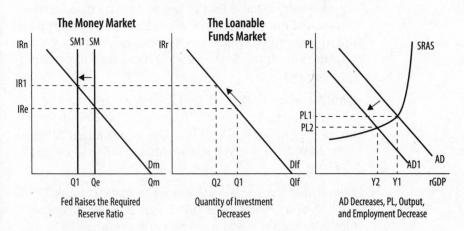

The Money Market   **The Loanable Funds Market**

Fed Raises the Required Reserve Ratio

Quantity of Investment Decreases

AD Decreases, PL, Output, and Employment Decrease

B. The Discount Rate. The discount rate (DR) is the interest rate that the Fed charges commercial banks for short-term loans borrowed from the Fed.

1. The Fed is known as the "lender of last resort" for commercial banks that have short-term liquidity needs. If banks have insufficient reserves, they have to borrow money to meet their required reserves at the end of a day of business, and the Fed is one place they can look to do such borrowing.

2. Banks that have a shortfall in their required reserves must make up that shortfall by borrowing funds from either another commercial bank or from the central bank.

   i. The rate banks charge one another for short-term loans between banks is called the federal funds rate (FFR) (because the funds the banks loan one another are typically kept at the Fed).

   ii. If a commercial bank is short on funds and cannot find another bank to lend it money to meet its reserve requirement, it may borrow from the Fed. The interest rate the Fed charges the commercial banks is called the discount rate (DR).

3. Typically, the DR will be around one percentage point higher than the FFR. Banks therefore prefer to borrow from one another to make up shortfalls in their required reserves.

   i. For example, assume that at the end of the day, Bank A has loaned out more than it expected to and determines that it is short $10 million in its required reserves. Bank A must borrow the $10 million to meet the legal reserve requirement.

   ii. Bank A can go to Bank Z, and if Bank Z has excess reserves equal to $10 million, it should be willing to lend the money to Bank A for a fee. The rate charged to Bank A by Bank Z for the $10 million loan is the federal funds rate.

   iii. Now instead, assume Bank A goes to Bank Z, Bank Y, Bank X, and several other banks, but they are all completely loaned out and have no excess reserves to lend. Bank A must now go to the Fed and borrow the $10 million it needs to meet its required reserves. The Fed charges Bank A a slightly higher fee known as the discount rate.

4. Changing the DR can have an expansionary or contractionary effect on the money supply.

    i.   Expansionary Monetary Policy—lower the DR. If the Fed wishes to increase the supply of money and lower the interest rate commercial banks charge their borrowers, it can reduce the DR, signalling to banks that it is cheaper and easier to borrow funds to meet their required reserves. Banks will be more willing to lend because they know obtaining needed reserves will be easier and cheaper.

    ii.   Contractionary Monetary Policy—raise the DR. A higher discount rate signals to banks that it is more costly to borrow funds from the Fed to meet their required reserves. Banks will be more conservative in their lending activity and will demand higher rates from their borrowers because they know that obtaining needed reserves will be more difficult and more costly.

5. Frequency of Use of the Discount Rate by the Federal Reserve. Historically, the Fed rarely changes the discount rate as a stand-alone tool of policy.

    i.   Typically, if the Fed engages in open-market operations aimed at lowering the federal funds rate (see below), it will lower the discount rate at the same time.

    ii.   If the Fed engages in open-market operations aimed at increasing the federal funds rate, it will raise the discount rate at the same time.

    iii.   The discount rate tends to be between 0.5 percent and 1 percent higher than the federal funds rate, signaling to banks that it is cheaper to borrow from one another than it is to borrow from the Fed, consistent with the Fed's view of itself as a "lender of last resort."

6. Impact of Changes in the Discount Rate in the Money Market

    i.   Expansionary Monetary Policy. If the Fed lowers the discount rate, the money supply increases and the interest rate falls.

ii. Contractionary Monetary Policy. If the Fed raises the discount rate, the money supply decreases and the interest rate rises.

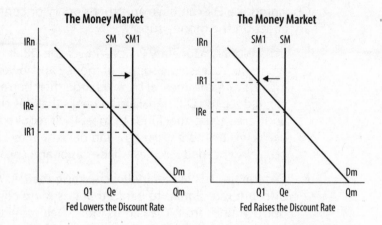

The Money Market — Fed Lowers the Discount Rate

The Money Market — Fed Raises the Discount Rate

C. Open-Market Operations (OMO). Open-market operations refers to the central bank's buying and selling of government bonds from commercial banks on the open market, aimed at increasing or decreasing the amount of excess reserves in the banking system, thereby influencing the federal funds rate, other interest rates, and the overall level of aggregate demand.

1. Commercial banks will lend money to both private sector borrowers (firms and households) and to the public sector (the government).

   i. Government bonds (also called treasury securities in the United States) are certificates of debt issued by the government that allow it to borrow from households, banks, international investors, and government institutions to finance budget deficits.

   ii. When an individual or a bank buys a government bond, it is lending money to the government, and in exchange receives an illiquid bond, a promise to pay in the future.

2. In the United States, at any given moment commercial banks may hold hundreds of billions of dollars worth of United States government bonds on their balance sheets.

    i.   Money loaned to the government through bond purchases may not be loaned to the private sector, thus, the more government bonds held by commercial banks and the public, the lower the level of excess reserves in the money market and the higher the level of interest.

   ii.   If the Fed wants to increase the supply of liquid money in the economy, it can simply buy bonds from the public and from commercial banks.

  iii.   If the Fed wants to decrease the supply of liquid money in the economy, it can engage in an open-market sale of government bonds.

3. OMO and the Federal Funds Rate. Government bonds held by commercial banks and the public are not part of the money supply, since bonds are not a form of money. When the Federal Reserve buys or sells these bonds, it affects the amount of excess reserves commercial banks have, thereby affecting the interest rate that commercial banks charge one another for short-term loans (the FFR) and thus the rates banks charge their customers.

    i.   Expansionary Monetary Policy—the Fed buys bonds on the open market. If the Fed wishes to lower the FFR, it should buy bonds from commercial banks and the public.

       ➤ An open-market purchase of bonds by the Fed will increase the supply of excess reserves in the banking system, as commercial banks sell their illiquid bonds to the Fed in exchange for liquid cash.

       ➤ With higher levels of excess reserves, banks will be willing to lend to one another at cheaper rates, so the FFR falls.

       ➤ Since it is now cheaper for banks to borrow from one another, they lower the rates they charge their customers, so interest rates across the economy decline, investment and interest-sensitive consumption increase, and aggregate demand shifts right.

➤ Expansionary OMO will increase the money supply, lower the interest rates, and thereby increase investment spending and stimulate AD, increase output, the price level, and employment.

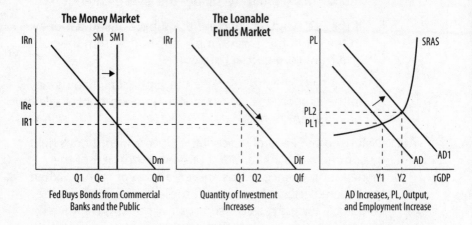

The Money Market
Fed Buys Bonds from Commercial Banks and the Public

The Loanable Funds Market
Quantity of Investment Increases

AD Increases, PL, Output, and Employment Increase

ii. Contractionary Monetary Policy—the Fed sells bonds on the open market. If the Fed wishes to raise the FFR, it should sell bonds to commercial banks and the public.

➤ An open-market sale of bonds by the Fed will decrease the supply of excess reserves in the banking system, as commercial banks buy illiquid bonds from the Fed in exchange for liquid cash.

➤ With lower levels of excess reserves, banks will be less willing to lend to one another at cheap rates, so the FFR rises.

➤ Since it is now more costly to borrow from one another, banks will raise the rates they charge their customers, so interest rates across the economy rise, investment and interest-sensitive consumption decline, and aggregate demand shifts left.

➤ Contractionary OMO will decrease the money supply, thereby increasing the interest rates, reducing investment spending, and contracting AD, which lowers output, the price level, and employment.

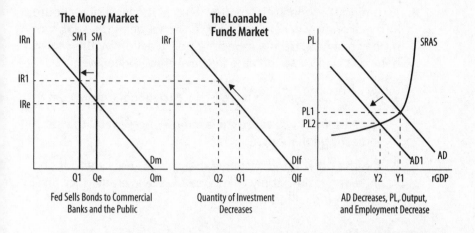

The Money Market

The Loanable Funds Market

Fed Sells Bonds to Commercial Banks and the Public

Quantity of Investment Decreases

AD Decreases, PL, Output, and Employment Decrease

Test Tip

Be familiar with the three tools of monetary policy. Many multiple-choice questions will test your understanding of these tools. The most commonly used is OMO, so expect several questions asking about the central bank's sale or purchase of government bonds, and be able to calculate the effect on the money supply of a bond sale or purchase of a particular size.

II. The Monetary Equation of Exchange

A. The Monetary Equation of Exchange (also called the quantity theory of money): $MV = PY$

1. M = the amount of money in circulation in an economy during a period of time.

2. V = the velocity of money, or the average number of transactions each unit of money will be used for in a given time period.

3. P = the average price level in the economy during a given time period.

4. Y = the level of output produced by the nation (real GDP).

B. Assuming the velocity of money (V) and the level of real output in the economy (Y) are constant, any change in the supply of money resulting from a monetary policy action by the central bank will lead to an increase in the average price level.

1. $P = \dfrac{MV}{Y}$. Without an increase in Y (national output), an increase in M will cause the average price level P to rise, indicating inflation.

2. On the other hand, if national output, Y, rises without an increase in the supply of money M, the average price level will fall, indicating deflation.

C. Implication for Monetary Policymakers. If policymakers pay attention to the formula MV = PY, they will be able to make policy decisions that balance economic growth and price stability effectively.

1. If money supply grows more rapidly than output growth, it will cause inflation.

2. If output grows more rapidly than the money supply, it will cause deflation.

3. The goal of policymakers, therefore, should be to increase the money supply at a rate that corresponds with the growth in national output. This ensures price-level stability (i.e., neither high inflation nor deflation).

Test Tip

The Monetary Equation of Exchange is infrequently tested on the AP exam. Still, it is important to know the implications of the theory for policymakers. For example, know that increasing the money supply rapidly will lead to inflation and little change in output.

PART VI

MACROECONOMIC POLICIES, INFLATION, AND UNEMPLOYMENT

Chapter

13

Fiscal and Monetary Policies

I. **Introduction to Fiscal Policy**

A. Fiscal Policy. *Fiscal policy* refers to the government's manipulation of levels of taxation and levels of government spending aimed at expanding or contracting the level of macroeconomic activity in the nation.

B. Expansionary Fiscal Policy. Any change in government spending or taxation that increases aggregate demand is considered an expansionary fiscal policy.

1. Reduction in Taxes. A tax cut stimulates aggregate demand in two ways:

   i. Households' disposable income is increased, leading to more consumption.

   ii. Firms have a greater incentive to expand output (assuming there is a reduction in business taxes), since they get to keep a greater percentage of their profits, leading to more investment.

2. Increase in Government Spending. An increase in a government's spending on goods and services stimulates aggregate demand in two ways:

   i. Government spending is a component of AD, so money spent on public goods, infrastructure, or any other domestic projects directly contributes to the total demand for output in a nation.

   ii. Government spending leads to new household income, which leads to further increases in consumption and investment by firms.

3. Effect of Expansionary Fiscal Policies on Economic Activity.

    i. When a government cuts taxes or increases its spending, AD shifts to the right, increasing output, employment, and the price level.

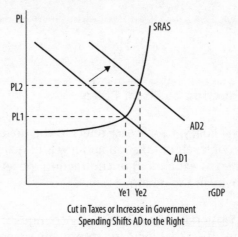

Cut in Taxes or Increase in Government
Spending Shifts AD to the Right

    ii. The degree to which a particular cut in taxes or increase in government spending shifts AD depends on the size of the spending multiplier in the case of an increase in government spending and the tax multiplier in the case of a decrease in taxes.

4. The tax multiplier. Indicates the degree to which a particular cut in taxes will increase total spending in a nation. The tax multiplier depends on the marginal propensities to consume and save.

    i. The tax multiplier, $t = \dfrac{-MPC}{MPS}$.

    ii. For example, assume in Country A, the marginal propensity to consume equals 0.8. The MPS is therefore equal to 1 − MPC = 0.2.

    ➤ The tax multiplier in this country, $t = \dfrac{-0.8}{0.2} = -4$.

➤ A particular decrease in taxes will lead to an increase in aggregate demand of four times the initial cut in taxes.

iii. Assume the government of Country A reduces taxes on households by $10 billion.

➤ The tax cut leads to an increase in disposable incomes of $10 billion, leading to an increase in consumption of $8 billion and an increase in savings of $2 billion.

➤ The increase in consumption of $8 billion leads to higher incomes for other households in the country, leading to more consumption and more savings.

➤ Using the tax multiplier of –4, we can conclude that a change in taxes of –$10 billion will ultimately lead to an increase in total spending (AD) of –10 × –4 = $40 billion.

5. Relative Effect of Tax Cuts and Increases in Government Spending on AD. The tax multiplier will always be smaller than the spending multiplier; therefore, an increase in spending of a certain amount will always have a greater effect than a tax cut of the same amount.

i. The spending multiplier, $k = \dfrac{1}{MPS}$. Using the same MPC and MPS numbers as our example above, Country A's spending multiplier would be $k = \dfrac{1}{0.2} = 5$.

ii. Assume that Country A decides to increase government spending by $10 billion, rather than passing a $10 billion tax cut.

➤ The effect of a $10 billion increase in government spending on AD will be 10 × 5 = $50 billion.

➤ The ultimate effect on aggregate demand will be greater when Country A increases government spending by $10 billion than when it cuts taxes by $10 billion.

iii. Rationale for the Different Sizes of the Tax and Spending Multipliers. Because a tax cut of a certain amount increases disposable income, and some of the increase is saved rather than spent on consumption, it will always have less of an effect than an increase in government spending of the same amount. Government spending is a direct injection into the circular flow; tax cuts are an indirect injection because they depend upon households spending some of the increase in disposable income to affect AD.

> *Be sure to know the difference between the spending multiplier and the tax multiplier. A common question on the AP exam is one on the relative impact of a particular change in taxes or government spending on GDP.*

6. Relative Effects of Tax Cuts and Government Spending Increases in the AD/AS Model.

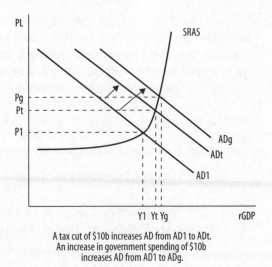

A tax cut of $10b increases AD from AD1 to ADt.
An increase in government spending of $10b
increases AD from AD1 to ADg.

C. Contractionary Fiscal Policy. Any change in government spending or taxation that reduces aggregate demand is considered a contractionary policy, and will lead to a lower price level and reduced output and employment.

1. Increase in Taxes. A tax increase will effect aggregate demand in the following two ways:

    i.   Households will have less disposable income, and therefore consumption will decrease.

    ii. Firms will be able to keep less of their profits (assuming there is an increase in business taxes), and therefore will be less willing to invest in new capital.

2. Decrease in Government Spending. A reduction in spending by government on public goods and services will reduce aggregate demand in the following ways:

    i.   There will be fewer employment opportunities in the public sector, reducing total demand for resources, goods, and services in the nation because government spending is a direct component of AD.

    ii. Households and private firms will experience lower incomes, reducing the level of private consumption and investment in the economy.

3. Effect of Contractionary Fiscal Policies on Economic Activity.

    i.   An increase in taxes or a decrease in government spending will contract the level of economic activity in the nation, reducing AD, output, and employment, putting downward pressure on the price level.

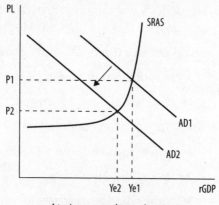

A tax increase or a decrease in government spending shifts AD to the left

ii. Raising taxes and decreasing government spending may be desirable in a nation producing beyond its full employment level with a high inflation rate.

iii. Raising taxes by a specific amount will have a weaker effect on AD than cutting government spending by the same amount. (Note that the tax multiplier and spending multiplier have the same relationship when influencing contractionary policy as they do in the case of expansionary policy.)

Knowing when certain policies will be most effective based on macroeconomic indicators such as the unemployment rate and the inflation rate is very important. Many questions will test whether you can determine the appropriate time for certain policies based on these factors.

II. Short-Run Effects of Fiscal and Monetary Policies

A. On Aggregate Demand. Following any change in fiscal or monetary policy by a government or central bank, aggregate demand will either increase or decrease, causing a change in the level of output, employment, and prices in the economy.

1. Expansionary Policies. Expansionary policies are to be used during periods of high unemployment or deflation. Expansionary policies include the following:

i. Fiscal policies (undertaken by government):

➤ a reduction in taxes;

➤ an increase in government spending.

ii. Monetary policies (undertaken by central bank):

➤ lower required reserve ratio;

➤ lower discount rate;

➤ open-market purchase of government bonds by the central bank.

iii. Expansionary policies should be used only during recessions. In the short run, any of the above policy actions will lead to the following:

➤ an increase in aggregate demand;

➤ an increase in the price level;

➤ and increase in employment (a decrease in unemployment);

➤ an increase in total output.

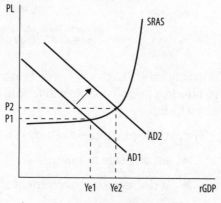

Expansionary Policies During a Recession

iv. Expansionary policies should not be used when an economy is already producing at or beyond its full employment level. If a government or central bank enacts expansionary policies in this situation, the following will happen:

➤ an increase in aggregate demand;

➤ little or no increase in employment;

➤ little or no increase in output;

➤ a large increase in the price level.

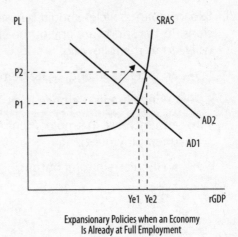

Expansionary Policies when an Economy
Is Already at Full Employment

2. Contractionary Policies. Contractionary policies are to be used during periods of high inflation. Contractionary policies include:

i. Fiscal policies (undertaken by government):

➤ an increase in taxes;

➤ a decrease in government spending.

ii. Monetary policies (undertaken by central bank):

➤ an increase in the required reserve ratio;

➤ an increase in the discount rate;

➤ an open-market sale of government bonds.

iii. Contractionary policies should be used only during periods of high inflation, when unemployment is already at or below the natural rate (NRU). In the short run, any of the above policies will lead to:

➤ a decrease in aggregate demand;

➤ a decrease in the level of national output;

➤ a decrease in employment;

➤ a decrease in the price level (or the inflation rate).

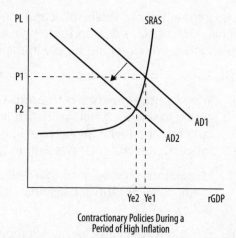

Contractionary Policies During a
Period of High Inflation

iv. Contractionary policies should not be used when an
economy is already producing at a level of output below
its full-employment level, or when the economy is in a
recession. If a government or central bank enacts contractionary policies in this situation, the following will
happen:

➤ a decrease in aggregate demand;

➤ a large increase in unemployment;

➤ a large decrease in national output;

➤ a small decrease in the price level.

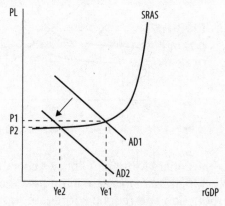

Contractionary Policies During a Recession

B. On Aggregate Supply. While fiscal and monetary policies are generally described as demand-side policies, they may also have an effect on aggregate supply in the short run.

1. The Crowding-Out Effect of Expansionary Fiscal Policy

   i. When a government has to borrow from the private sector to finance a budget deficit resulting from a tax cut combined with an increase in government spending, interest rates may be driven up in the private sector.

   ii. Higher interest rates lead to a reduction in private investment, reducing the expansionary effect of the fiscal policy.

   iii. Effect of Crowding Out on Aggregate Supply. Crowding out can increase the costs faced by private firms, and have the following negative effects:

   ➤ reduction in aggregate supply;

   ➤ reduction in output;

   ➤ reduction in employment;

   ➤ increase in the price level.

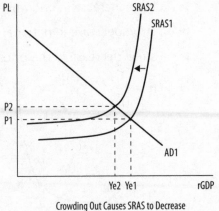

Crowding Out Causes SRAS to Decrease

2. Expansionary Monetary Policy's Effect on Aggregate Supply. Much as an increase in interest rates can add to costs of production and reduce aggregate supply, a policy that leads

to a lower interest rate reduces firms' costs and may increase aggregate supply.

i.   When a central bank expands the money supply, the corresponding increase in bank reserves puts downward pressure on interest rates across the economy.

ii. Firms find it cheaper to borrow funds for investment, and their interest payments are lower than they would be otherwise.

iii. Firms will hire more workers to operate their new capital equipment, and may also pass the lower interest payments onto consumers as lower prices.

iv. Expansionary monetary policy can have positive supply-side effects, including:

  ➤ an increase in aggregate supply;

  ➤ an increase in output;

  ➤ an increase in employment;

  ➤ a decrease in the price level.

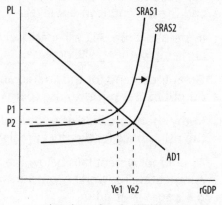

Lower Interest Rates Cause SRAS to Increase

v.   While monetary policy may impact AS, it is more commonly considered a demand-side policy; therefore, being able to explain and illustrate its effects on AD is more important than analyzing the supply-side effects.

III. Long-Run Effects of Fiscal and Monetary Policies

A. From Short Run to Long Run in Macroeconomics. Recall that in the long run, all wages and prices are variable in an economy.

1. In periods of high inflation and low unemployment, workers' real wages will decline as prices rise and in the long run they will demand higher nominal wages, increasing costs to firms.

2. In periods of deflation and high unemployment, workers' real wages will increase as prices fall and due to the high unemployment, they will be willing to accept lower nominal wages, reducing costs to firms.

B. Expansionary Demand-Side Policies and Long-Run Output. Following the implementation of any expansionary demand-side policy, there will be a short-run change in output, price level, and employment, but in the long run output will always return to its full-employment level.

1. Assume a government or central bank undertakes expansionary policies aimed at increasing aggregate demand beyond the full-employment level.

   i. In the short run, AD will increase, output, price level, and employment will increase.

   ii. Greater demand for the limited amount of the nation's output causes prices to rise (demand-pull inflation).

   iii. In the short run, workers' nominal wages are fixed, so the rising price level reduces real wages.

   iv. As unemployment falls below the natural rate, increased competition for workers puts upward pressure on nominal wages over time.

   v. In the long run, nominal wages will rise as increasingly scarce workers demand higher wages to accommodate for the rising price level.

   vi. The higher wage rate raises the costs of hiring workers to firms, forcing a reduction in employment and even higher prices being passed on to consumers.

vii. In the long run, output and employment will return to the full-employment level, and inflation will increase, possibly leading to an inflationary spiral.

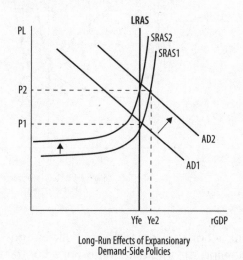

Long-Run Effects of Expansionary
Demand-Side Policies

2. Effect on Long-Run Output. Expansionary demand-side policies by themselves will have no effect on the long-run level of full-employment output in a nation.

3. However, if the demand-side policy also has positive supply-side effects, it may increase the full-employment level of output in the long run.

   i. Expansionary Monetary Policy's Effect on Long-Run Aggregate Supply: Since lower interest rates lead to more investment, expansionary monetary policy may lead to economic growth, increasing the level of output the economy is capable of producing at in the long run.

   ii. Increased investment leads to more AD, but also shifts AS outward, as seen below.

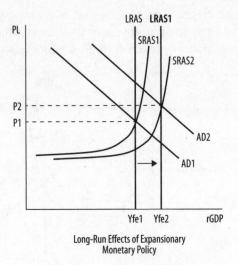

Long-Run Effects of Expansionary
Monetary Policy

C. Contractionary Demand-Side Policies and Long-Run Output: Following the implementation of a contractionary demand side policy, there will be a short-run change in output, but in the long run output will return to its full-employment level.

1. Assume a government or central bank undertakes contractionary policies that reduce aggregate demand to a level below the full-employment level of output.

   i. In the short run, AD will decrease, reducing the level of output, employment, and prices in the economy.

   ii. The lower overall demand for output puts downward pressure on prices, but since wages are fixed in the short run, deflation will be minimal.

   iii. Over time, as unemployment rises and prices begin to fall, workers' real wages increase, and the high number of unemployed workers begins to exert downward pressure on nominal wages.

   iv. As nominal wages begin to fall, firms find it cheaper to hire workers, and employment and output begin to recover.

v. In the long run, output and employment will return to the long-run full-employment level, but the economy will be at a lower overall price level.

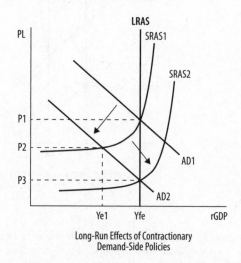

Long-Run Effects of Contractionary
Demand-Side Policies

2. Effect on Long-Run Output. Contractionary demand-side policies will have no effect on long-run output by themselves, but if they also affect the productive capacity of the economy, they may be harmful to the nation's production possibilities curve in the long run.

3. If a contractionary fiscal policy reduces spending on the nation's productive resources, such as infrastructure, education, and health, then the productivity of the nation's resources may be reduced and the long-run level of output will decline.

    i. If a contractionary fiscal policy leads to higher interest rates and firms reduce their investments in new capital, the nation's capital stock may decline, reducing the nation's productive capacity and reducing the long-run level of output.

    ii. If any contractionary demand-side policy also reduces the level of aggregate supply by reducing the quality or the quantity of the nation's resources, it could lower the nation's long-run competitiveness and productive capacity.

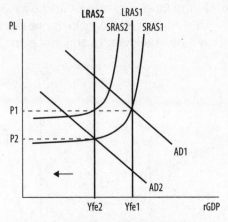

Long-Run Effects of Contractionary Policies
that Reduce Nation's Productive Capacity

In the free-response section you may be asked to show the short-run and the long-run effects of particular fiscal or monetary policies. Such analysis is simple if you remember that in the long run an economy will always return to its full-employment level of output regardless of the demand-side policies undertaken by government and the central bank.

IV. Mixing Fiscal, Monetary, Demand-Side, and Supply-Side Policies

A. During a Recession. Depending on the depth of the recession an economy finds itself in, fiscal policy may be more effective than monetary policy at restoring output and employment.

1. Monetary policy may be ineffective during a recession:

   i. Investment demand may be highly inelastic.

      ➤ Lower interest rates, in theory, lead to a greater level of private investment.

      ➤ The responsiveness of firms to changes in the interest rate depends on the level of investment demand and the elasticity (sensitivity) of investment demand.

➤ If firms are not responsive to changes in interest rates, then expansionary monetary policies will not affect aggregate demand.

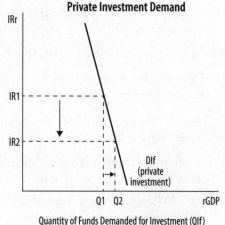

Private Investment Demand

Quantity of Funds Demanded for Investment (QIf)

Inelastic investment demand makes
expansionary monetary policy ineffective.

ii. Interest rates cannot fall below zero percent.

➤ Expansionary monetary policy lowers the interest rates that banks charge one another for short-term loans (the federal funds rate).

➤ The interest rate cannot go below zero percent, so if the rate is near zero percent, and investment spending is still low, further increases in the money supply will have no further effect on the level of investment spending in the economy. Beginning in 2008, the Federal Reserve faced this dilemma. Quantitative easing describes efforts to further increase the money supply even when interest rates cannot fall any further.

➤ In the loanable funds market, in which the firms' demand for investment is low during a recession and savings is high due to economic uncertainty, there may be an excess supply of loanable funds due to the fact that interest rates cannot fall below zero percent.

➤ In extremely troublesome economic times, banks may hold lots of excess reserves out of precautionary motives and frustrate monetary policy.

➤ In such a case, monetary policy will be ineffective at stimulating aggregate demand and promoting recovery.

2. Fiscal policies may be more effective during a recession.

i. Fiscal policy, unlike monetary, directly injects money into the circular flow and therefore moves AD rightward.

ii. Therefore, when an economy is in a deep recession, expansionary fiscal policy may be required.

iii. The following are further justifications for the use of fiscal policy during a recession:

➤ When savings is high and investment is low, governments can borrow from the public at low interest rates.

➤ Tax cuts and increases in government spending can be justified because private spending (consumption and investment) is depressed, meaning the crowding-out effect is less severe.

➤ With high unemployment rates, targeted government spending can have a powerful impact on output and employment, without putting upward pressure on inflation.

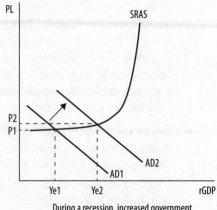

During a recession, increased government spending increases output, and employment, without causing inflation.

> ➤ Because interest rates are low during a recession, the future interest burden on the nation will be lower than if the government were to borrow during periods of higher interest rates.

3. Policy Mix During Recession. First try monetary, then fiscal. If monetary policy proves ineffective at stimulating AD and increasing employment, a government should then turn to fiscal policy. Often monetary policies can fix minor downturns. The more severe the recession, the more likely fiscal stimulus will be needed with the expansion of the money supply to restore full employment.

B. During a Period of Inflation. Depending on the degree of inflation in the economy, a combination of monetary and fiscal policies can be employed to bring the price level down.

1. One of the objectives of macroeconomic policy is low and stable inflation. Typically, keeping inflation under control is the central bank's job; therefore, monetary policy is usually used to maintain a low rate of inflation.

   i.   In most countries, an inflation rate of between two and three percent is desired.

   ii. If policymakers are concerned about rising inflation, they will typically respond by reducing the money supply.

   iii. An open-market sale of government bonds by the central bank reduces excess reserves in the banking system and brings interest rates up.

   iv. Higher interest rates reduce the incentive to invest and consume and increase the incentive to save.

   v.   Reduced investment and consumption and increased savings will reduce AD, bringing down the price level and moving the economy back to its full-employment level of output.

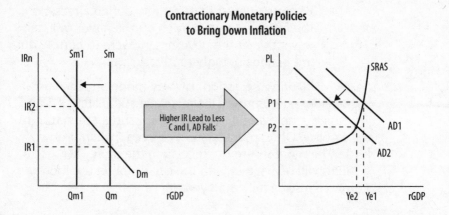

Contractionary Monetary Policies to Bring Down Inflation

2. If monetary policy proves ineffective at bringing down inflation, contractionary fiscal policies may be required.

   i. If inflation rates are high, monetary policy may prove ineffective because:

   ➤ The central bank influences only nominal interest rates, while private households and firms respond to the real interest rate. Recall that the higher the inflation rate, the further apart real and nominal interest rates will be.

   ➤ With high inflation, a higher nominal interest rate will not deter investment and consumption, as private spenders have a strong incentive to spend now during a period of high inflation, since postponing purchases means money will be worth less in the future.

   ➤ Expectations of continued inflation create an even stronger incentive to spend, so unless the private sector expects inflation to decline, they will continue to spend, fueling ever-increasing inflation.

   ➤ Because of the effect inflation has on the behavior of private households and firms, contractionary monetary policy will be ineffective if it does not drive up interest rates to a level high enough to deter investment and spending.

ii. To support the central bank, a government can implement contractionary fiscal policies to combat inflation.

➤ Higher taxes on investment and on household income will force households and firms to reduce their spending.

➤ Cuts in public spending will reduce the level of aggregate demand in the economy and bring down prices and output to a more reasonable level.

3. If inflation in the economy is caused by rising costs of production (known as cost push inflation), then policymakers face a difficult challenge in deciding which to use, monetary or fiscal. The best response to stagflation may be simply to wait until resource costs have fallen.

Inflation and Unemployment

I. Types of Inflation

A. Demand-Pull Inflation. Inflation caused by an increase in the level of overall demand for a nation's output is known as demand-pull inflation.

1. When any of the components of AD increase (C, I, G, or Xn) without an increase in the productive capacity of the nation (AS), there is upward pressure on the price level.

2. The increased competition among consumers for the increasingly scarce amount of output forces prices to rise.

3. The degree of inflation resulting from rising demand depends on the nation's equilibrium level of output when demand starts to rise.

   i. When an economy is in equilibrium below full employment, an increase in AD will have only minor effects on the price level, because

   ➤ Unemployment is high and workers can be hired to meet the growing demand without driving up wages.

   ➤ Unused resources such as empty factories and idle machines can be brought into use with little to no rise in production costs.

   ➤ The economy may have been experiencing deflation to begin with, so rising demand may lead to very low inflation, which is more desirable than deflation.

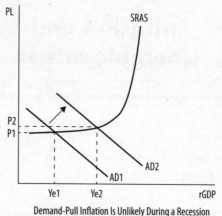

Demand-Pull Inflation Is Unlikely During a Recession

ii. When an economy is in equilibrium at or close to full employment, demand-pull inflation is more likely to occur when AD rises because

➤ Labor markets are already very tight, so there are fewer available unemployed workers for firms to hire as they increase their output. Additional units of labor that firms hire are less productive and often more expensive.

➤ As the economy approaches its potential output level, older and less efficient machinery needs to be brought into service. This causes production costs to rise.

➤ Inflation rates are most likely already positive when demand starts to increase, causing them to rise beyond a desirable level.

iii. When an economy is in equilibrium above full employment, increases in AD are likely to produce the most extreme versions of demand-pull inflation.

➤ Because no more workers are available, firms must bid against one another for existing labor resources.

➤ All machinery and other capital is already in use, so output cannot rise.

➤ The increased demand only pushes up prices because it cannot induce any more output.

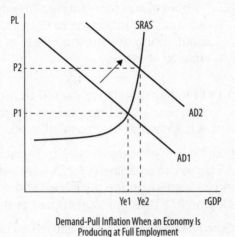

Demand-Pull Inflation When an Economy Is
Producing at Full Employment

4. Methods for Reducing Demand-Pull Inflation.

i. Contractionary Fiscal Policies. Although raising taxes and reducing spending is never a popular policy position for a government in power, such responses can be effective, because:

➤ higher taxes reduce household disposable income and therefore consumption;

➤ reduced government expenditures lowers the level of AD and frees up resources to meet the growing private sector demand (and could therefore promote a growth in aggregate supply).

ii. Contractionary Monetary Policies. Central bank action is likely to be the first response to high inflation. Contractionary monetary policies have several advantages over fiscal policies.

➤ They can be enacted swiftly, as the central bank can engage in an open-market sale of bonds within a matter of weeks of rising inflation fears.

➤ Central bankers are often unelected and politically independent, and therefore do not require government support (nor does monetary policy put the reputation of any sitting political leaders at risk).

    iii. Both fiscal and monetary policies are contractionary demand-side responses to demand-pull inflation and should bring down the increase in average price level if enacted effectively.

B. Cost-Push Inflation. Inflation caused by an increase in the nation's resource costs or a decrease in the productivity of those resources is known as cost-push inflation.

  1. If any of the determinants of aggregate supply change, the AS curve can decrease (or shift leftward, graphically), causing an increase in the price level and an increase in unemployment, a phenomenon known as stagflation.

  2. Cost-push inflation can be caused by any of the following:

    i. An increase in the average wage rate. Wages are the primary cost of production for firms in most developed nations. Higher wages mean firms must reduce their employment of labor and pass higher costs on to consumers as higher prices.

    ii. An increase in the price of raw materials. Primary commodities' prices can have a significant effect on the level of aggregate supply in an economy. Higher input costs force firms to reduce employment and pass higher prices on to consumers.

    iii. An increase in energy and transportation costs. Higher oil, gas or coal prices will make energy and transportation costs rise, forcing firms to cut costs by laying off workers, and to pass higher costs on to consumers as higher prices.

    iv. Higher business taxes. Taxes are a cost to firms imposed by the government. An increase in taxes on firms may force them to cut costs by laying off workers, and to pass higher taxes on to consumers as higher prices.

  3. A change in any of the above determinants of AS will shift the SRAS curve to the left, causing cost-push inflation and rising unemployment.

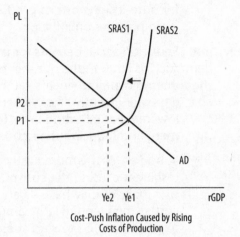

Cost-Push Inflation Caused by Rising
Costs of Production

4. Methods for Reducing Cost-Push Inflation.

   i. Contractionary Demand-Side Policies. Higher interest rates, higher taxes, or reduced government spending can be effective at bringing down inflation caused by rising prices. However, such policies have a major disadvantage:

      ➤ Since AD shifts to the left and the economy is already producing below its full-employment level of output, unemployment will increase.

      ➤ The economy will fall further into recession, which may require further stimulus from the government or central bank to remedy.

  ii. Expansionary demand-side policies may fix the unemployment problem, but will worsen the inflation problem.

 iii. Expansionary supply-side policies, if effective, can correct both the unemployment and the inflation problem resulting from cost-push inflation.

      ➤ Lowering business taxes will reduce the costs to firms and increase employment and lower prices.

      ➤ Reducing minimum wages will make hiring workers more attractive to firms and help compensate for other rising costs of production, putting downward pressure on inflation.

➤ Reducing social benefits for unemployed workers, such as limiting the number of months over which unemployment benefits can be collected, creates a greater incentive for workers to accept jobs for lower wages, allowing firms to increase employment and reducing their costs of production.

➤ Subsidies for the more costly energy or primary resources causing the cost-push inflation, although such policies may have a very high opportunity cost as they require large amounts of tax revenues to be reallocated toward subsidies for firms.

➤ Just waiting. In some cases, energy and commodity prices fluctuate dramatically in the short run, but in the long run such costs tend to decline as abruptly as they rise. Sometimes before any major fiscal, monetary, or supply-side action is taken, a government may be better off just waiting for costs to fall on their own.

➤ The proper policy response to cost-push inflation is not a settled matter for macroeconomists. It is in part because of these factors that stagflation is perhaps the most frustrating macroeconomic problem for policymakers.

Test Tip

Cost-push inflation is the trickiest for policymakers to fix using traditional demand-side policies, since any change in AD alone will worsen either the inflation problem (if AD increases) or the unemployment problem (if AD decreases). Therefore, supply-side policies may be most appropriate.

II. **The Phillips Curve: Short-Run vs. Long-Run Relationships Between Inflation and Unemployment**

A. The Short-Run Phillips Curve. As can be seen in much of the analysis in this and previous chapters, there appears to be a trade-off in the short run between the level of inflation in an economy and the level of unemployment.

1. Any change in aggregate demand will inversely affect the inflation rate and the unemployment rate, *ceteris paribus.*

   i.   If AD increases and there is no change in aggregate supply, demand-pull inflation is accompanied by an increase in output and employment, and thus a decrease in the unemployment rate.

   ii. If AD decreases and there is no change in aggregate supply, the inflation rate will decrease (or even become negative), while output and employment fall, thus increasing the unemployment rate.

   iii. It is because of the upward slope of SRAS that this trade-off exists. However, SRAS is only an indirect depiction of this because unemployment must be inferred from output level.

2. The short-run trade-off between unemployment and inflation can be more directly illustrated in a simple diagram known as the Phillips Curve.

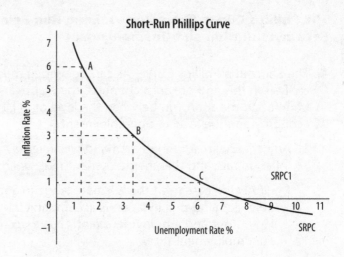

Short-Run Phillips Curve

i. Each of the three points, A, B, and C, corresponds with a different level of inflation and unemployment.

➤ At point A, the economy has relatively high inflation (6 percent) and very low unemployment (1 percent).

➤ At point B, both inflation and unemployment are around 3 percent.

➤ At point C a very low inflation rate (1 percent). corresponds with a higher rate of unemployment (6 percent).

➤ As can be seen, at unemployment rates of greater than 8 percent, this economy experiences negative inflation (or deflation).

ii. The inverse relationship between inflation and unemployment means that a Phillips Curve is downward sloping, showing that as unemployment rises, inflation falls, and vice versa.

iii. An accurately drawn Phillips Curve should intersect the horizontal axis at some point, indicating that deflation is possible if unemployment becomes high enough.

3. Explanation for the Short-Run Phillips Curve Relationship. Anytime both unemployment and inflation change in op-

posite directions, there is a movement along the short-run Phillips Curve.

i. An increase in aggregate demand causes an increase in inflation and a decrease in unemployment, corresponding with a movement up and to the left along the short-run Phillips Curve.

ii. A decrease in aggregate demand causes a decrease in inflation and an increase in unemployment, corresponding with a movement down and to the right along the short-run Phillips Curve.

iii. Any shift in AD, *ceteris paribus*, causes a movement along the short-run Phillips Curve because it causes a movement along a given SRAS curve.

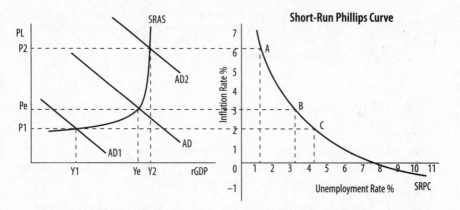

iv. In the diagram above, assume aggregate demand begins at AD in the graph on the left.

➤ At the intersection of AD and SRAS, there is an inflation rate of around 3 percent and an unemployment rate of around 3 percent, corresponding with the point B on the short-run Phillips Curve.

➤ A decrease in aggregate demand to AD1 causes national output and employment to fall, causing a decrease in the price level (or in the inflation rate) from 3 percent to 2 percent and an increase in unemployment from 3 percent to 4.2 percent. This corresponds with a movement along the short-run Phillips Curve to point C.

➤ An increase in aggregate demand to AD2 causes national output and employment to rise, causing inflation to increase from 3% to 6% and unemployment to fall from 3% to 1.5%. This corresponds with a movement along the short run Phillips Curve to point A.

➤ Anything that causes the AD curve to shift causes a movement along a given SRAS curve and along the short run Phillips Curve (but in the opposite direction), since unemployment and inflation always change in opposite directions in the short-run.

It is helpful to think of the short-run Phillips Curve as a mirror image of the short-run aggregate supply curve. Anything that shifts SRAS left will shift the SRPC right. Anything that increases SRAS will shift SRPC to the left.

B. The Long-Run Phillips Curve. In the long run, there is no trade-off between inflation and unemployment.

1. Changes in aggregate demand will affect an economy's short-run level of output, but in the long run, output always returns to the full-employment level

2. Since a nation will always produce at its full-employment level of output in the long run, it will always return to the level of unemployment that corresponds with full-employment output, otherwise known as the natural rate of unemployment.

3. When wages adjust to changes in the price level, the SRAS curve shifts in or out (depending whether there is inflation or deflation). When SRAS shifts, the short-run Phillips Curve shifts in the opposite direction.

4. For example, assume an economy is producing at full employment and there is an increase in aggregate demand.

i. In the short run, inflation increases and unemployment falls. There is a movement up and to the left along the short-run Phillips Curve.

ii. Over time, the low unemployment rate and high inflation rate leads to workers demanding higher nominal wages to compensate for the higher rate of inflation.

iii. Higher nominal wages force firms to reduce employment and pass higher costs onto consumers as even higher prices, shown as a leftward shift of SRAS.

iv. In the long run, once wages have adjusted to the higher price level, output returns to its full-employment level and inflation is higher than before.

v. Unemployment returns to its full employment level, or its natural rate, and inflation is at a new, higher level than before AD ever increased. This is shown as a rightward shift of the short-run Phillips Curve.

vi. Note that the change in wages caused movement of SRAS and short-run Phillips Curve but in opposite directions.

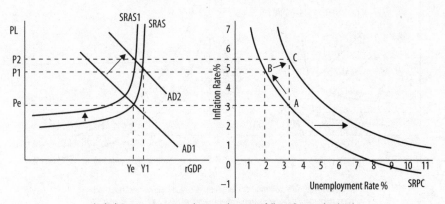

In the long run, an economy always produces at its full-employment level and returns to its natural rate of unemployment, which in this economy is around 3%.

5. Now assume the economy is producing at full employment and there is a decline in aggregate demand.

i. In the short run output falls, employment falls, and the inflation rate falls. There is movement down and to the left along the SRAS, so there is a movement down and to the right along the short-run Phillips Curve.

ii. Over time, the high unemployment rate and the falling inflation rate puts downward pressure on nominal wage rates, as increased competition for limited jobs forces workers to accept lower wages.

iii. Lower nominal wages allow firms to hire more workers and pass the savings on to consumer as lower prices, shown as a rightward shift in SRAS.

iv. In the long run, once wages have adjusted to the lower price level, output returns to its full-employment level and inflation is at a lower rate than before the fall in AD.

v. Unemployment returns to its *natural rate* and there is a lower rate of inflation. This corresponds with a leftward shift of the short-run Phillips Curve.

vi. Note again that the change in wages caused movement of SRAS and short-run Phillips Curve but in opposite directions.

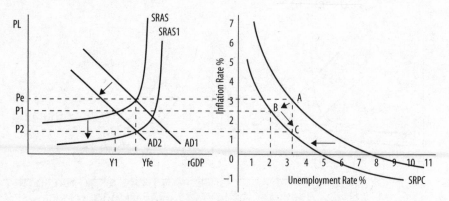

In the long run, an economy always produces at its full-employment level and returns to its natural rate of unemployment, which in this economy is around 3%.

6. Regardless of whether AD increases or decreases in the short run, in the long run an economy will always produce at its full-employment level of output due to the perfect flexibility of wages and prices, which will fluctuate based on the level of aggregate demand in the economy.

7. In the long run, therefore, there is no trade-off between inflation and unemployment.

   i. Just as there is a long-run aggregate supply curve that is vertical at the full-employment level of output, there is a long-run Phillips Curve which is vertical at the natural rate of unemployment.

   ii. Since output will always return to its full-employment level once wages and prices have adjusted in the long run, unemployment will always return to its *natural rate* in the long run.

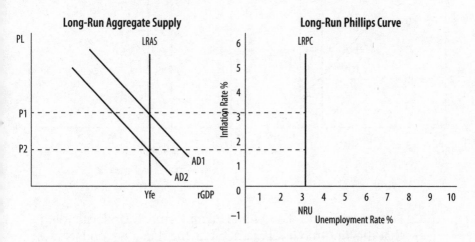

   iii. In the graph above, it can be seen that regardless of the level of aggregate demand in the economy, output and unemployment will return to the NRU in the long run.

8. LRAS and LRPC are mirror images.

   i. Some of the factors that shift a nation's long-run aggregate supply to the right will shift its long-run Phillips Curve to the left, allowing the nation to produce at a lower natural rate of unemployment. Factors that could cause an increase in LRAS and also a leftward shift of the LRPC include:

      ➤ increase in the productivity of labor;

      ➤ improved education;

> ➤ greater capital stock, requiring more labor;

> ➤ improved health care system;

> ➤ improved skills training for the structurally unemployed;

> ➤ any other factor that reduces the structural and or the frictional rates in unemployment in the nation.

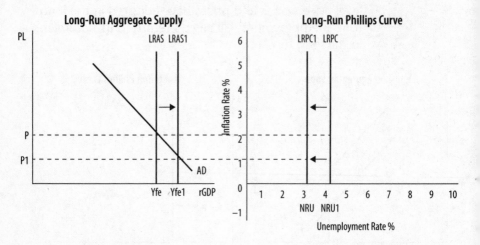

C. Policies to Reduce Long-Run Unemployment. Understanding that the long-run level of unemployment in a nation includes structural and frictional unemployment, a government can undertake certain policies that reduce the number of long-term unemployed.

1. Education. Investments in education aimed at equipping the nation's people with skills for the future economy, rather than that of the past, will ensure that in the long run the number of people whose skills do match with the demand for labor among employers will be lower than it otherwise would.

2. Research and Development. Governments that finance research and development of new technologies and scientific research assure that private firms in their economies will enjoy new areas in which to invest over time, increasing the demand for skilled labor in the long run.

3. Infrastructure. Infrastructure, including roads, bridges, ports, energy grids, transportation, and communication systems, are known as public goods, meaning without government provision they would go under-provided by the free market. A government that invests in modern and efficient infrastructure will attract investment from domestic and foreign firms, keeping demand for labor high and the long-run level of unemployment low.

4. Health. A healthy workforce is a productive workforce. A country with a publicly provided healthcare system is more attractive to firms looking to invest in production facilities, since the firms' burden for the health care of their workers is less. The corresponding demand for labor will keep the natural rate of unemployment lower than it might be otherwise.

III. The Role of Expectations

A. The speed with which an economy will return to its full-employment level of output following a disruption to demand (i.e., AD increases or decreases) depends on whether individuals in the economy (households and firms) make decisions based only on present economic conditions or they consider their expectations of future economic conditions.

1. Keynesian Economic Theory. According to the Keynesian school of thought, households and firms are relatively slow to respond to changing macroeconomic conditions. Therefore, government responses aimed at increasing or decreasing aggregate demand to promote economic objectives can be quite effective.

   i. For example, if AD falls,

      ➤ unemployment rises and output falls, but wages and prices are slow to adjust ("sticky downward") because households base their wage demands on current and past economic conditions, not on the expectation of future price levels and employment prospects.

➤ an economy will remain stuck in a demand-deficient recession until aggregate demand recovers.

➤ expansionary fiscal and monetary policies can help such an economy return to full employment quicker than it would be able to on its own.

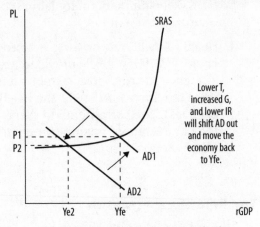

Sticky wages and prices mean demand-side policies are needed to fix an economy in recession.

  ii. If policies are undertaken to increase AD,

➤ unemployment falls and output increases, but wages and prices are slow to adjust. Therefore, inflation increases, but not to a large extent.

➤ the economy is able to produce at a higher level of output, indicating that expansionary policies succeeded at promoting economic growth and at increasing employment.

  iii. In both cases, the use of expansionary demand-side policies (Keynesian policies) improves upon the macroeconomic outcomes that would be achieved if the economy were left entirely to its own devices.

2. Rational Expectations Theory (RET). RET says that rational households and firms will base their decisions regarding the employment and use of their resources on their expecta-

tions of future economic conditions more than on past and present economic conditions. These theorists believe that an economy will be quick to self-correct following shocks to aggregate demand because wages and other input costs are very flexible and that policy action to restore full employment is often unnecessary.

i.   For example, if AD falls

➤   unemployment rises and output falls. Households and firms will *expect* prices to continue to fall, and will therefore adjust their wage demands based on their poor expectations of future price levels and employment opportunities.

➤   wages will be quick to adjust downward during a demand-deficient recession, encouraging firms to hire workers, quickly moving the economy back to full employment. In such a case, expansionary fiscal and monetary policies are not needed, since the process of *self-correction* occurs swiftly due to individuals who adjust their behavior based on their future expectations.

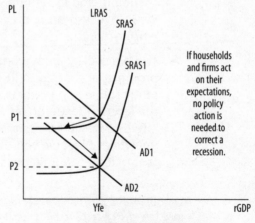

Under RET, a fall in AD leads to a fall in wages and a quick return to Yfe.

ii. On the other hand, according to the rational expectations theory, if there is an increase in AD when an economy is producing at its full-employment level,

➤ unemployment falls and output increases in the short run, but with the expectation of inflation households quickly demand higher nominal wages.

➤ the increased nominal wage rate forces firms to reduce employment and raise prices, moving the economy quickly back to its full-employment level, with a higher inflation rate.

iii. In both cases above, demand-side policies will only interfere with the efficient functioning of the nation's economy following a change in aggregate demand, and therefore demand-management monetary and fiscal policies are ineffective at improving upon what the free market is capable of on its own.

➤ The role of expectations in macroeconomic policy decisions shows that expansionary demand-side policies (such as lower taxes, more government spending, and lower interest rates) are ultimately ineffective at promoting economic growth and employment.

➤ The best policy a government or central bank can promote, according to RET, is one that is consistently stable and predictable. Constantly changing the levels of taxes, government spending, and interest rates in an economy will only contribute to uncertainty and worsen the economic fluctuations that macroeconomic policymakers wish to avoid.

Questions about rational expectations theory are rare on the multiple-choice section, but you can expect one or two on the exam. Typically, such a question will ask how a particular change in monetary or fiscal policy will affect the level of output if the change is anticipated by households and firms. You should understand that if changes are expected, then they will have no effect on real output in the long run, since individuals will adjust their behavior before the change takes effect.

PART VII
ECONOMIC GROWTH AND PRODUCTIVITY

Sources of Economic Growth and Productivity

Chapter

15

I. Economic Growth—Definition, Measurement, and Illustration

A. *Economic growth* is an increase in the potential total output of goods and services in a nation over time. Growth is measured by the change in productive capacity of an economy between one period of time and another.

1. Growth can be positive. If a nation's GDP increases between one period and the next, the economy has experienced growth.

2. Growth can be negative. If a nation's GDP decreases between one period and the next, the economy has contracted, and is experiencing recession.

3. Growth can be measured as the change in real GDP or real GDP per capita.

B. Economic growth is considered a desirable macroeconomic objective because

1. as output grows, income rises and the nation is richer;

2. a greater level of output generally means the nation's people have access to more and a greater variety of goods and services—new combinations of goods that previously lay outside the country's PPC are now attainable;

3. if the rate of economic growth exceeds the rate of population growth, the average person in a nation also becomes richer.

C. Measuring Economic Growth

1. Growth is stated as a percentage change in real GDP from one period of time to the next

    i. Growth rate = $\dfrac{GDP2 - GDP1}{GDP1} \times 100$, where GDP2 is the real gross domestic product from one year and GDP1 is the gross domestic product during the previous year.

2. For example, assume Country A's real GDP increases from $150 billion in 2010 to $165 billion in 2011:

    i. Country A's growth rate = $\dfrac{165 - 150}{150} = \dfrac{15}{150} \times 100 = 10\%$.

    ii. The real value of Country A's output between 2010 and 2011 increased by 10%.

3. Next, assume Country A's real GDP decreased from $165 billion to $140 billion between 2011 and 2012:

    i. Country A's growth rate =
        $\dfrac{140 - 165}{165} = \dfrac{-25}{165} \times 100 = 15.15\%$.

    ii. The real value of Country A's output decreased by 15.15% between 2011 and 2012. Country A's real output fell, indicating the country experienced a recession.

D. Illustrating Economic Growth

1. In the Business Cycle and PCC Diagrams. Economic growth can be illustrated in these two diagrams.

2. In the AD/AS Model. Both short-run and long-run economic growth can be illustrated in an AD/AS diagram.

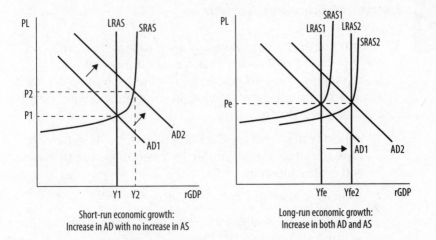

Short-run economic growth:
Increase in AD with no increase in AS

Long-run economic growth:
Increase in both AD and AS

i. In the graph on the left, AD increases without an increase in AS.

   ➤ In the short run, GDP increases beyond the full-employment level, but over time, wages will increase and output will return to the full-employment level

   ➤ An increase in AD leads to only a short-run increase in GDP, which is not sustainable.

ii. In the graph on the right, both AD and AS increase.

   ➤ The nation's productive capacity increases; therefore, the full-employment level of national output increases.

   ➤ An increase in both AD and AS leads to sustainable long-run economic growth.

Practice calculating the rate of economic growth using simple numbers as in this chapter. It is not uncommon to have to do this calculation in both the multiple-choice and the free-response sections.

II. Sources of Economic Growth

A. Investment in Human Capital. *Human capital* is the improvement to the value of labor that is created through education, training, knowledge, and health. Better human capital is achieved through improvements in the education and health of a nation's workforce.

1. Importance of Human Capital. Improvements in human capital lead to a more productive workforce, greater output, and higher incomes.

2. Sources of Human Capital Growth

   i. Education. A highly effective education system assures that all members of society, rich and poor, learn the skills that will allow them to become productive members of the nation's workforce.

      ➤ Math and Science. Skills in math and science are particularly valuable in a rich modern economy, in which jobs in engineering, finance, business, and computer technologies are in greater demand.

      ➤ Technology. An education system that teaches students how to work with various technologies will prepare a workforce with the skills to work in a modern economy.

      ➤ Low-Skilled Labor. In less-developed countries in which the primary and secondary sectors are still the dominant sources of employment, education in math, science, and technology is important, but so are the less-skilled workers who are able to function in a factory or manufacturing facility.

   ii. Health. An educated workforce is not enough. A healthy workforce is also needed to ensure an economy achieves growth in its output and income.

      ➤ Healthy workers are more productive than unhealthy workers.

➤ Good health means long life, allowing workers to contribute to economic activity until later in their lives than if they were less healthy.

➤ Good health makes a country more attractive to firms looking for a place to invest in capital. More capital investment increases the productive capacity of the nation and increases the level of economic activity.

iii. Skills. Similar to education, a growing economy requires workers whose skills align with what is in demand in the labor markets.

➤ Workers with a certain skill set are not guaranteed employment for life in a rapidly changing economy. As the structure of the nation's economy evolves, the skills workers need to contribute to growth change.

➤ Giving workers new skills is the responsibility of both the private sector and the public sector. Employed workers should be trained by their employers with skills that bring value to the firm's production and therefore contribute to national output. Workers who are unemployed should be given skills by the government that get them back into the workforce, allowing them to contribute to economic growth.

3. Impact of Improved Human Capital on National Output

i. Anything that improves the education, health, and skill sets of the nation's workforce will make labor more productive, allowing the nation's firms to produce more output at a lower cost.

ii. Aggregate supply increases due to improved human capital.

iii. In addition, since workers are more productive, their real incomes should be higher and the overall level of aggregate demand should increase as well.

iv. Improved human capital increases both AD and AS, leading to long-run economic growth.

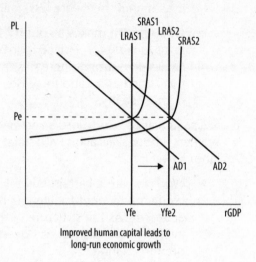

Improved human capital leads to
long-run economic growth

B. Investment in Physical Capital. *Physical capital* refers to tools and machinery employed in the production of goods or services. Factories, robots, computers, buildings, and other such equipment are all considered physical capital.

1. Typically, private investment by firms increases the stock of the physical capital in a nation.

   i. All production requires labor, land, and capital. When firms invest in new capital goods, the productivity of the other resources (land and labor) increases and firms are able to produce more output.

   ii. Increased investment by a firm increases that firm's individual output, and when the level of investment increases across a nation it increases national output.

2. The level of investment by firms in a nation is determined by several factors:

   i. Interest rates. There is an inverse relationship between the interest rate and the level of private investment because interest is the cost of borrowing to buy capital goods.

ii. Business confidence and expectations. When firms are confident about the future level of demand for their products, they are more likely to invest in capital now.

iii. Technology. When new technologies and innovations are marketed that have the potential of increasing firms' revenues or reducing their costs, investment will increase.

iv. Government regulation and taxes. Reduced regulation of the private sector and lower business taxes are likely to increase the level of private investment.

3. Impact of Investment on National Output. As the stock of capital in a nation increases, the productivity of the nation's existing resources improves and the long-run level of national output increases.

   i. Since investment is a component of aggregate demand, there will also be a growth in the total level of spending in the nation.

   ii. Investment in capital increases both short-run and long-run aggregate supply.

   iii. Both AD and AS increase, allowing the economy to grow not only in the short run, but in the long run as well.

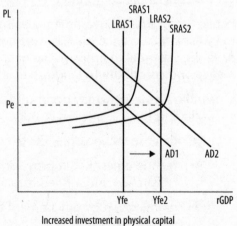

Increased investment in physical capital increases both AD and AS

C. Research and Development and Technological Progress. Many of the improvements in technology, education, and capital that lead to improved productivity and increased investment are the result of research and development (R&D) by both the private and the public sectors.

1. Private Sector R&D. Private firms have a strong incentive to invest in R&D in their individual sectors of the economy.

   i. When intellectual property rights enjoy legal protection (through a system of patents or copyrights), private firms stand to gain monopolies in new areas of technology developed as a result of their own research.

   ii. Private sector R&D has resulted in countless technologies that have increased the productivity of labor and land, including both simple and advanced technologies such as:

      ➤ the cotton gin

      ➤ the combustion engine

      ➤ vaccinations

      ➤ chemical fertilizers

      ➤ nuclear energy

      ➤ personal computing technologies

2. Public Sector R&D. Government also has a strong incentive to invest in R&D, since the new technologies developed have the potential to improve the nation's economic performance and contribute to long-run economic growth.

   i. Public sector R&D may occur through many channels, including:

      ➤ defense technologies developed for the military;

      ➤ technologies that improve agricultural output researched and funded through state universities;

      ➤ grants given by government to support research of various types;

      ➤ spinoff technologies created as by-products of a nation's space program (NASA in the United States);

➤ publicly funded research in various fields undertaken by public universities.

ii. When a technology is researched and developed by the
public sector, it may become the exclusive possession of
the government for a period of time, or its patents may
be handed to a private sector firm, or the technology
may be made available to the public.

3. The impact of R&D on the Nation's Economy

i. Without constant research and development being undertaken by both the private and the public sectors, the
level of technology in a country will become stagnant
and out of date, reducing the potential for long-run
economic growth.

ii. However, through continual renewal in the types and
variety of technologies available to a nation's producers
and consumers, there is likely to be continued growth in
both AD and AS, helping the economy grow its level of
output in both the short run and long run.

III. **Growth Policy**

A. Macroeconomic policies that increase both AD and AS are most
effective at promoting long-run economic growth in a nation.

1. Demand-Side Policies. Fiscal policies that increase only AD
will be ineffective at achieving economic growth in the long
run. However, if fiscal policies increase both AD and AS,
long-run growth can be achieved.

i. Increases in government spending on projects that do
not contribute to the nation's infrastructure or capital
stock can be highly wasteful and will lead only to short-
run growth and inflation.

ii. However, expansionary fiscal policies that increase the
level of infrastructure or capital stock will contribute to
the productivity of the nation's resources and promote
long-run economic growth and price stability.

2. Supply-Side Policies. Expansionary monetary policies and fiscal policies that increase aggregate supply as well as aggregate demand will promote long-run economic growth

   i. Expansionary monetary policy, which lowers interest rates and increases the level of investment, will increase AD, but may also increase the nation's capital stock and shift AS to the right, promoting long-run economic growth.

   ii. Expansionary demand-side policies involving lower taxes on investment or other incentives to encourage the acquisition of new capital by the private sector will promote long-run growth.

B. Provision of Public Goods by the Government

1. Education and health improve human capital and allow for a more productive workforce; therefore, government should support or provide both education and health for the nation's households.

   i. Education

     ➤ Public schools provide an educational foundation in most countries through the secondary level.

     ➤ Public universities provide free or subsidized tertiary education, further improving the skills of the nation's workforce and contributing to long-run growth.

   ii. Health

     ➤ A national health care system assures that all citizens, rich or poor, are guaranteed a certain level of health care. Many developed economies offer households at least a basic level of health care.

     ➤ A system that provides health care to the poor and the elderly assures that when private health coverage is out of reach or when a household slips into poverty, a basic level of health care is still achievable.

2. A government's provision of infrastructure promotes efficiency in the private sector and ensures economic growth is possible.

   i. Transportation Infrastructure

     ➤ Highways allow for the efficient transportation of goods around the nation, reducing transportation costs for firms and encouraging more private sector investment.

     ➤ Rail and air transportation infrastructure require public funding, and both improve the efficiency with which people and cargo are transported around a nation.

   ii. Other Infrastructure. Other types of infrastructure a government can provide or support to promote long-run economic growth include:

     ➤ sanitation systems, such as water, sewer, and food safety;

     ➤ communication infrastructure;

     ➤ law enforcement and judicial infrastructure;

     ➤ energy infrastructure.

Test Tip

Be sure to be able to distinguish between short-run growth (caused by an increase in AD only) and long-run growth (achieved when both AD and AS increase). Short-run growth is unsustainable unless there is a corresponding increase in the productivity or the quantity of the nation's resources.

PART VIII

OPEN ECONOMY: INTERNATIONAL TRADE AND FINANCE

Balance of Payments Accounts

Introduction to the Balance of Payments

A. A nation's balance of payment measures the exchanges that take place in three separate accounts:

1. The current account. Measures the net flow of funds exchanged for goods and services into one nation from all other nations. It also records monetary gifts or grants that flow into or out of a country.

2. The financial account. Measures the net flow of funds for investment in real assets (such as factories or office buildings) or financial assets (such as stocks and bonds) into a nation from the rest of the world.

3. Official reserves. To balance the two accounts in the balance of payments, a country's official foreign exchange reserves measures the net effect of all the money flows from the other accounts. This measure captures whether there is a net buildup of foreign currency held in a country over a period of time.

B. The balance of payments (BoP) will always equal zero when the three accounts above are added together.

1. If a country's current account is in surplus (greater than zero), then its capital account and official reserves, when added together, will be in deficit (less than zero).

2. If a country has a current account deficit (less than zero), then its capital account and official reserves will be positive, and the BoP taken as a whole will equal zero.

II. The Current Account

A. The current account measures the flow of goods, services, and income between the residents of one nation and the residents of other nations.

B. The current account balance is also referred to as the balance of trade. It can be divided into four separate components, outlined below.

C. If the sum of the four components is greater than zero, then a nation has a current account surplus, which means the total income from foreigners' spending on its output is greater than the its own spending on foreign output. In other words, that country exports more than it imports. On the other hand, a current account deficit results when residents of a nation spend more on imported goods and services than they earn from their sale of exports to the rest of the world. This is also known as a trade deficit.

D. The measure of net exports (the Xn component of aggregate demand) is the same as the current account.

E. The four components of a nation's current account balance are:

1. Balance of trade in goods. This measures the spending by consumers and firms in one nation on another nation's goods (both consumer and capital goods) as well as spending by consumers in the rest of world on the recording nation's goods.

    i. Goods Credits (+). Goods exported count as a credit in the current account, since they require that foreigners make payments to the exporting nation. Note that the export of both consumer and capital goods count as credits in the current account.

    ii. Goods Debits (−). Spending by domestic consumers on goods produced in foreign nations count as debits in the current account, since they require a payment to foreign producers.

2. Balance of trade in services. Services refer to non-tangible purchases such as tourism, banking, consulting, legal services, and transportation. Services can be "imported" and "exported," although there will be no physical transportation of a product involved.

   i. Services Credits (+). Services bought by foreigners, either within the nation or from abroad, count as a credit in the current account, since they require that a foreign consumer makes a payment to a domestic producer.

   ii. Services Debits (–). Services consumed by domestic households that were purchased from foreigners are a debit in the current account since they require a payment to a foreign producer.

3. Income balance. The transfer of incomes earned by citizens of one country from activities in another country back to the income earner's country of origin are also measured in the current account. This includes the wage income earned by a country's citizens for employment by foreign companies abroad.

   i. Income Credits (+). This includes wages earned by a country's workers employed abroad that are sent home, interest on a country's residents' savings and investments in foreign banks and financial markets, and dividends earned abroad from domestic investors purchasing stocks in foreign firms. Each of these transactions requires that foreigners make payments to residents of the country in question, so are counted as a credit in the country's current account.

   ii. Income Debits (–). Wages paid by firms in one country to foreign workers in that country that are sent abroad, count as a debit in the current account. In addition, interest paid to foreign savers in domestic banks and dividends paid to foreign shareholders in a domestic company are all considered "leakages" and therefore are counted as a negative (debit) in the current account.

4. Current transfer balance. A transfer refers to a payment made from one nation to another that is not in exchange for any good or service, such as a gift or a grant. Transfers are

divided into two categories: official transfers are payments from one government to another, sometimes known as "aid," and private transfers are payments made by citizens of one country to residents of any other country. Current transfers can be recorded as either a credit or a debit in the current account.

i. Transfer Credits (+). Official and private transfers from foreign governments or households to the government or individuals in a country count as a credit in the current account. All such transfers require a payment from foreigners to domestic stakeholders, increasing the level of disposable income at home and reducing it in the foreign country.

ii. Transfer Debits (−). Official and private transfers by the government or individuals within a nation to foreign governments or households count as a debit in the current account. Both transfers require a payment from domestic stakeholders to interests abroad, increasing disposable income abroad while reducing it at home.

F. When all the credits and debits from each of the components of the current account are added together, they will either equal a positive number or a negative number.

1. A positive current account balance is called a trade surplus. If a country has a trade surplus, it means it receives more payments in its current account from the rest of the world than it makes in payments to other countries and that Xn is positive.

2. A negative current account balance is called a trade deficit. If a country has a trade deficit, it has made more payments for goods, services, income, and transfers to the rest of the world than it has received from abroad and that Xn is negative.

Test Tip

A country's balance of payments is always meant to be in balance, naturally. This means that if there is a surplus in one account there must be a deficit in the other account. Any discrepancy is accounted for as a change in foreign exchange reserves.

III. The Financial Account (formerly known as the Capital Account)

A. The financial account measures the exchanges between a nation and the rest of the world involving ownership of financial and real assets.

B. Foreigners may buy and sell a country's assets, including real estate, factories, office buildings, and other factors of production. Such transactions are recorded in the financial account because they involve the ownership of assets, not the purchase of the nation's output of goods or services. Assets purchased in the financial account include things that won't be brought back to the purchaser's home country, unlike goods and services.

C. In addition to physical assets, the financial account also measures the exchange of financial assets such as companies' stocks and government bonds.

D. The financial account measures two types of investments:

1. *Direct investment* means acquiring a significant ownership stake in a foreign business. *Foreign direct investment* refers to the buying and selling of a minimum of 10 percent of a company's shares by a foreign investor in the domestic economy or by a domestic investor in another nation's economy. Whether direct investment counts as a positive or a negative in the financial account depends on who is buying what.

   i. Direct Investments Abroad. Investors from one country may buy or sell ownership stakes in foreign firms.

      ➤ Credits (+). When domestic investors sell shares in foreign firms there is an inflow of financial capital, moving the financial account toward the positive.

      ➤ Debits (–). When domestic investors acquire an ownership stake in foreign companies there is an outflow of financial capital, which moves the financial account toward the negative.

        ii. Direct Investments at Home. Foreign investors may buy or sell ownership stakes in domestic firms.

           ➤ Credits (+). When foreign investment in shares of domestic firms increases, there is a net inflow of financial capital, moving the financial account toward the positive.

           ➤ Debits (–). When foreigners sell their ownership stake in domestic firms to domestic investors, there is an outflow of financial capital, moving the financial account toward the negative.

2. Portfolio Investment Abroad. Portfolio investment measures the investments of foreigners in businesses in the domestic economy and domestic investors investing in businesses and government debt abroad. The difference between portfolio investment and foreign direct investment is that, to be considered FDI, the investment must result in a minimum of 10 percent equity ownership in the foreign firm. Equity ownership of less than 10 percent is considered portfolio investment. The recording of these transactions affects the financial account in exactly the same way as for FDI.

        i. Portfolio Investment Abroad. The money spent by domestic investors in foreign equity and debt counts as an asset to the investor's home country and a liability to the foreign country.

           ➤ Credits (+). When investors sell those assets, foreigners make a payment to the domestic investor, so there is an addition (+) to the financial account.

           ➤ Debits (–). When domestic investors buy foreign assets, there is a subtraction (–) in the financial account, since it requires a payment to a foreign stakeholder.

        ii. Portfolio Investment at Home. The money spent by foreigners on domestic stocks, shares, and bonds counts as a liability for the home country and as an asset to foreigners.

➤ Credits (+). A foreign investor buying domestic securities makes a payment to the home country, creating a positive entry in the financial account.

➤ Debits (–). When the foreign investor sells his domestic securities, there is a subtraction from the financial account, since domestic firms or the government must make a payment to the foreign investor.

3. *Other investment* usually refers to loans made by banks to foreign borrowers or money saved in banks across national borders.

   i. Loans from domestic banks to foreign borrowers and savings by domestic households in foreign banks count as assets for the home country, since foreign interests owe money to domestic interests.

   ➤ Credits (+). When a foreign borrower pays back a loan to a domestic bank, it counts as a positive inflow in the financial account since it requires a payment from foreigners to domestic interest.

   ➤ Debits (–). When a domestic bank makes a loan abroad, it counts as an outflow (negative inflow) in the financial account since it requires a payment to a foreigner.

   ii. Domestic borrowing from foreign banks and foreign savings in domestic banks are considered liabilities for the home nation, an asset for the foreign nation.

   ➤ Credits (+). Money borrowed from a foreign bank counts as a positive for the domestic financial account, since it requires a payment from abroad to a domestic interest.

   ➤ Debits (–). When a loan is repaid to a foreign bank, there is an outflow of financial capital, resulting in a shift toward the negative in the financial account.

The AP exam only recently began referring to the account measuring the flow of financial transactions and ownership of assets abroad as the **financial account.** *In the past it was known as the* **capital account.** *You should be familiar with both terms and realize that they may be used interchangeably on future exams.*

IV. Official Reserves Account

A. *Foreign exchange reserves* refer to the assets of other nations held by a country's central bank. Reserves consist primarily of foreign financial assets such as government bonds and foreign currency.

B. When the flow of money into a country in a given year from its exchanges in the current and financial accounts exceeds the flow of money out of the country, the difference is added to the central bank's official reserves of foreign exchange.

C. If there is a net outflow of money in a year, the difference is made up by a withdrawal from the central bank's reserves of foreign exchange, indicated by a decrease in the amount of foreign reserves held by the central bank.

   1. A net deficit in the current and financial accounts actually results in an *inflow* (thus, a positive sign) in the official reserves account, since the deficit country *must sell* its reserves of foreign currency to make up for the net deficit.

   2. If a country has a net balance of payment surplus, then the change in the foreign exchange reserves is recorded as a negative since the country's ownership of assets denominated in foreign currencies actually increases each year its current and financial accounts added together are positive.

D. Purpose of Foreign Exchange Reserves

   1. The presence of foreign exchange reserves in a nation's central bank allows the government to draw on these reserves

to intervene in the market for their nation's currency to influence the exchange rate, or to balance out the financial account in years when the current and financial accounts do not balance out.

2. Additionally, foreign assets can be sold and converted to the domestic currency to finance government spending in times of fiscal need.

E. Practically speaking, the current and financial accounts for a given country will almost exactly equal each other in magnitude (absolute value) in every year. They will have opposite signs (one will be positive while the other is negative). Thus the foreign exchange reserves component is to be regarded as minor compared to financial and current accounts.

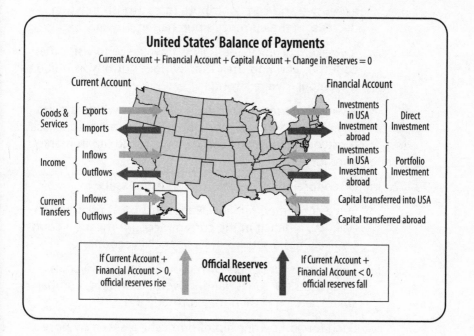

United States' Balance of Payments

Current Account + Financial Account + Capital Account + Change in Reserves = 0

Current Account

Goods & Services { Exports / Imports

Income { Inflows / Outflows

Current Transfers { Inflows / Outflows

Financial Account

Investments in USA / Investment abroad } Direct Investment

Investments in USA / Investment abroad } Portfolio Investment

Capital transferred into USA

Capital transferred abroad

If Current Account + Financial Account > 0, official reserves rise

Official Reserves Account

If Current Account + Financial Account < 0, official reserves fall

V. **Consequences of Imbalances in the Balance of Payments**

A. Consequences of a Current Account Deficit. If a nation runs a persistent deficit in its current account (i.e., imports more than it exports), the following consequences may result:

1. Depreciation of the currency.

    i.   A primary determinant of exchange rates is the demand for exports and imports.

    ii. If domestic consumers demand more imports than foreigners demand of the home country's exports, then the value of the domestic currency will fall relative to foreign currencies.

    iii. A weaker currency makes imported raw materials more expensive and can contribute to cost-push inflation, decreasing the currency's purchasing power.

    iv. A weaker currency also harms travelers who visit other countries and find their money does not buy as much as it would if it were stronger.

    v.   A weaker currency does help producers within a country who sell some of their goods to foreigners, because those goods now will carry a lower price tag in markets abroad.

2. Increased foreign ownership of domestic assets.

    i.   Since current and financial accounts must be in rough balance, a deficit in the current account means a country likely has a surplus in its financial account.

    ii. This means foreigners own more of the home country's assets (factories, land, government debt, company shares, etc. . . .) than they formerly did.

    iii. Such foreign ownership of domestic assets may pose a threat to the economic sovereignty (freedom) of the deficit country.

3. Higher interest rates that slow long-run growth.

    i.   In order to offset the inflationary effects of a weak currency, a country's central bank may try to strengthen the currency by raising interest rates to attract foreign capital to the country.

ii. A higher interest rate will negatively affect domestic investment by firms, slowing growth in the nation's capital stock over time.

iii. Less capital makes the country less productive and less competitive in the global economy, slowing growth and reducing income for domestic households and firms.

4. Increased indebtedness to foreign countries.

i. A current account deficit is offset by a financial account surplus. One of the domestic assets foreign investors will demand is government bonds.

ii. Increased selling of bonds by the government to foreign investors increases the amount of national debt held by foreigners.

iii. When a government has large amounts of foreign-held debt, it must pay interest on that debt, meaning taxpayer money is being paid to foreigners, reducing the government's ability to spend as much on domestic projects like infrastructure, education, and health care.

B. Consequences of a Current Account Surplus. If a nation runs persistent surpluses in its current account, the following consequences may result:

1. Appreciation of the currency.

i. Since a current account surplus means the country is exporting more than it is importing, foreigners are demanding more of the surplus nation's currency, putting upward pressure on the value of the exchange rate.

ii. An appreciating currency will harm producers in the export sector and could reduce domestic employment.

iii. A stronger currency will help restore balance in the current account, but has several adverse effects on domestic interests as well, and may lead to uncertainty among international investors who will think twice about investing in the surplus country's economy.

    iv. Stronger currencies do, however, help consumers because imported goods feel cheaper. In addition, citizens wishing to travel abroad will find those trips more affordable due to the appreciated currency.

  2. Increased domestic ownership of foreign assets.

    i. A surplus in the current account is usually offset by a deficit in the financial account.

    ii. Domestic investors will increase their ownership of foreign assets (stocks, government debt, real estate, and factories), meaning there is a net outflow of capital from the country.

  3. Reduced standards of living for the nation's households.

    i. If a nation exports a large proportion of its total output, there is less left over for domestic housholds to consume.

    ii. While a current account surplus may be good for employment, it is often bad for domestic consumption, since the money earned from exported goods and services is not entirely spent on imports.

  4. Possibility of protectionism imposed by foreign governments.

    i. Foreign governments unhappy with the trade imbalance with the surplus nation may threaten to impose protectionist measures on the exporting nation's goods.

    ii. Such measures, including tariffs, quotas, or subsidies for producers in the deficit country, will undermine the surplus nation's comparative advantage and reduce employment and output.

C. Methods for Correcting an Imbalance in the Balance of Payments. Both a current account deficit and a current account surplus have several affects on a nation, some of which are undesirable. Therefore, a government or central bank may undertake policies to reduce deficits and surpluses when they exist.

1. Exchange Rate Intervention

   i. By intervening in the foreign exchange market a government or central bank can try to either appreciate or depreciate the country's currency.

   ii. To correct a current account deficit, the government would wish to devalue (weaken) its currency, making its exports more attractive to foreigners.

   iii. To correct a trade surplus, the government would wish to revalue (strengthen) its currency, making imports cheaper to domestic consumers.

2. The Use of Monetary Policies

   i. Contractionary monetary policies would raise interest rates and lead to an inflow of capital in the financial account, appreciating the currency and reducing a trade surplus.

   ii. Expansionary monetary policies would lower interest rates and lead to an outflow of capital in the financial account, depreciating the currency and reducing a trade deficit

3. The Use of Protectionism

   i. *Protectionism* refers to the use of tariffs, quotas, or subsidies aimed at increasing competitiveness of domestic producers against foreign producers.

   ii. Tariffs are taxes on imports. A tariff will raise the cost of imported goods and allow domestic producers to sell their products at a higher price at home.

   iii. A quota is a physical limitation on the quantity of a certain imported good. Quotas create shortages of certain products in the domestic market, forcing the price and the domestic quantity supplied to increase.

   iv. Subsidies for domestic producers are a payment from the government per unit produced. They reduce domestic costs of production and therefore reduce the price of domestic goods, making imports less attractive.

v. Typically, protectionist measures are used to increase the current account of a country.

vi. If a country has a large trade surplus, reducing any of the above protections will make imports more competitive and reduce the current account surplus.

vii. Often these measures result in retaliatory measures being adopted by trading partners, making them counterproductive.

viii. Economists often view these measures as inefficient because they tend to block trade.

The terms surplus *and* deficit *often have positive and negative connotations associated with them, but this should not be the case. A trade surplus, for example, has as many downsides as it does benefits for a nation.*

Foreign Exchange Market

Introduction to the Foreign Exchange Market

A. Just like any commodity, currencies are traded between buyers and sellers in markets. There are almost as many different currencies as there are countries in the world. The exchange rate (value of any particular currency relative to any other currency) is determined in the market for that country's currency relative to the other currency in question.

1. A currency's exchange rate only tells us the value of that currency relative to another currency to which it is being compared.

2. The value of one currency in terms of another will always be the reciprocal of the other currency's value in terms of the original currency. For instance, assume the following: One US dollar = one half British pound.

   i. The dollar exchange rate is $1 = £0.5.

   ii. The pound exchange rate is the reciprocal of 0.5, so

   $$£1 = \frac{1}{0.5} = \$2.$$

3. If the value of a currency increases in terms of another currency, the first currency is said to have appreciated.

4. If the value of a currency decreases in terms of another currency, the first currency is said to have depreciated.

5. In markets that relate two currencies to one another, if one currency appreciates, the other must depreciate. This follows directly from the fact that the two exchange rates are reciprocals.

B. There are many markets for foreign exchange in the world, although the major forex markets, as they are called, are in New York, London, Tokyo, Hong Kong, and Singapore.

II. Demand and Supply for Foreign Exchange

A. In any forex market, buyers and sellers meet to exchange currencies from various countries for currencies from various other countries.

B. The demand for any particular currency represents the quantity of the currency demanded at a series of exchange rates in a particular period of time by those holding other currencies who may wish to buy goods, services, resources, or real or financial assets from the country whose currency is demanded. For example:

1. The demand for Mexican pesos in the US dollar/peso market represents the following:

    i. American households who wish to buy goods produced in Mexico;

    ii. American households who wish to travel to Mexico;

    iii. American firms who wish to buy capital equipment produced in Mexico;

    iv. American firms who wish to buy raw materials originating in Mexico;

    v. American investors who wish to purchase Mexican real or financial assets;

    vi. The American government, which may wish to hold Mexican pesos as an asset in its central bank;

    vii. Anyone else who holds American dollars but now wishes to use them to "buy" (convert them into) Mexican pesos.

2. The demand for a currency is downward sloping, showing an inverse relationship between the currency's exchange

rate and the quantity demanded by foreigners. Using the peso as an example, this is explained by the following:

i.   When a currency's exchange rate falls, goods, services, resources, and assets in that country appear cheaper to foreigners. Therefore, the quantity demanded of the currency by foreign households, firms, investors, and governments increases.

ii. A weaker peso (which costs less dollars to buy) will increase the quantity of pesos demanded in the United States.

3. The Demand for a Currency in a Forex Diagram.

i.   The demand for a foreign currency in a nation can be illustrated in a forex market diagram:

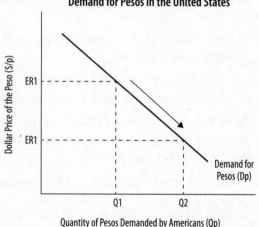

Demand for Pesos in the United States

ii. A decrease in the dollar-to-peso exchange rate leads to a movement along the demand curve for pesos. American would wish to buy more Mexican goods, services, resources, and assets if the price of the peso in terms of dollars were to fall.

iii. A change in the exchange rate, *ceteris paribus*, leads to a movement along the demand curve for a currency.

C. The supply of any currency in a forex market represents the willingness and ability of people in the country whose currency is represented to supply the currency to foreigners at a series of exchange rates in a particular period of time.

1. Pesos in the United States are supplied by the following:

   i. Mexican households who exchange their pesos in order to buy American goods;

   ii. Mexican households who wish to travel to the United States;

   iii. Mexican firms who wish to buy capital goods produced in the United States;

   iv. Mexican firms who wish to buy raw materials originating in the United States;

   v. Mexican investors who wish to purchase American real or financial assets;

   vi. The Mexican government, which may wish to hold US dollars as an asset;

   vii. Anyone else who holds Mexican pesos and is willing to "sell" them for (convert them into) American dollars.

2. Notice that the supply of pesos in the United States comes from the same interests as those who demand pesos, only their Mexican counterparts.

3. The suppliers of pesos are also the demanders of dollars in Mexico's dollar market. Just as there is a market for pesos in the United States, there is also a market for US dollars in Mexico

4. Supply of a currency is upward sloping, demonstrating a direct relationship between the exchange rate and the quantity of the currency supplied. Using the peso as an example, this relationship is explained by the following:

   i. When the exchange rate is low (the peso is weak), Mexicans will be willing and able to supply fewer pesos to the peso market because American goods will appear more expensive. Mexicans will demand fewer American goods and therefore exchange fewer pesos for dollars.

ii. When the peso appreciates (gets stronger) relative to the dollar, Mexicans will buy more American goods, which requires them to exchange more pesos for dollars, increasing the quantity of pesos available in the United States.

5. Supply of a Currency in a Forex Diagram

i. Supply of a currency in a nation can be illustrated in a forex diagram

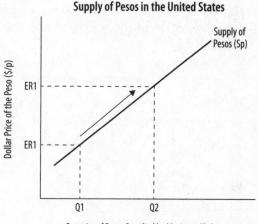

Supply of Pesos in the United States

Quantity of Pesos Supplied by Mexicans (Qp)

ii. An increase in the dollar/peso exchange rate leads to a movement along the peso supply curve in the United States. Mexicans would wish to buy more American goods when the peso is strong; therefore, there will be more pesos supplied to the United States market for pesos.

iii. A change in the exchange rate, *ceteris paribus*, leads to a movement along the supply curve for a currency.

Questions in both the multiple-choice and the free-response sections often ask you to identify the effect a change in government or central bank policy will have on the country's exchange rate in foreign exchange markets. Answering such a question requires you "connect the dots" and determine how the fiscal or monetary policy in question will affect either domestic inflation, incomes, or interest rates, and then determine how that change will affect demand for or supply of the country's currency on foreign exchange markets. Such questions are very common.

D. Equilibrium Exchange Rate in the Forex Market

1. The equilibrium exchange rate for a currency occurs at the intersection of the supply of and the demand for the currency.

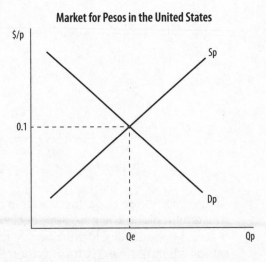

i. In the graph above, the equilibrium exchange rate for pesos ($0.1) occurs at the intersection of supply and demand. One peso costs Americans only $0.10, or ten cents.

ii. The vertical, price axis is labeled $/p, short for "dollars per peso." In the market for pesos, the "p" must be the denominator and the "$" the numerator. Mislabeling the vertical axis in a forex diagram is a common mistake.

However, remembering that this is similar to markets for simple goods may help. In this market for pesos, the vertical axis is the price of one peso in dollars just the same as in the market for apples the vertical axis is the price of one apple in dollars and in the market for cars the vertical axis is the price of one car in dollars.

2. The market for a particular currency has a parallel market for the currency to which it is being compared. For example, the graph above shows the market for pesos in terms of the dollar. There is a parallel market for dollars in terms of pesos.

   i. Anything that causes a change in one forex market is accompanied by a change in the parallel market. The dollar market in Mexico shows the supply of dollars from Americans, the demand for dollars from Mexicans, and the peso per dollar exchange rate, as seen below:

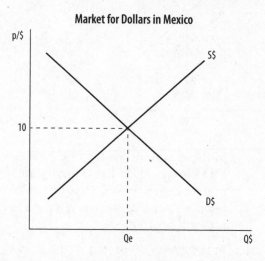

Market for Dollars in Mexico

   ii. In the graph above, the equilibrium exchange rate for dollars in Mexico (10p) occurs at the intersection of supply and demand. One dollar costs 10 Mexican pesos.

   iii. Notice that the peso-to-dollar exchange rate (10) is the reciprocal of the dollar-to-peso exchange rate (0.1):

$$10 = \frac{1}{0.1}.$$

    iv. The vertical, price axis in the dollar market is labeled p/$ for "pesos per dollar." It requires 10 Mexican pesos to purchase one US dollar's worth of American goods. Again, this is the market for dollars, so the vertical axis should be the price of one dollar in terms of whatever will be used to buy that dollar, in this case, pesos.

3. A change in one market is accompanied by a simultaneous change in the other market. For example, if Americans demand more pesos to buy more Mexican products, they are supplying dollars in order to do this. Both the peso and the dollar exchange rate will change, but in opposite directions.

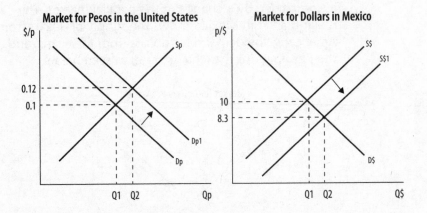

    i. In the graph on the left, the increase in demand for Mexican goods in the United States leads to an increase in demand for pesos, causing the peso to appreciate relative to the dollar. Now, a peso is worth 12 cents rather than 10 cents.

    ii. In the graph on the right, the inflow of dollars into Mexico causes the supply of dollars to increase and the dollar to depreciate relative to the peso. Now a dollar is worth only 8.3 pesos rather than 10 pesos.

    iii. Notice that the new exchange rates are reciprocals of one another: $8.3 = \dfrac{1}{0.12}$.

4. Anything that increases the demand for one currency will increase the supply of the other.

5. Anything that reduces demand for one currency will reduce the supply of another.

6. Whenever one currency appreciates, the other currency depreciates, and vice versa.

Test Tip

Labels in foreign exchange market diagrams are tricky and should be given particular attention when drawing these graphs. The vertical, price axis should always make clear that the price of a currency is expressed in terms of another currency. The dollar market in Europe, for example, should be labeled The price of dollars in terms of euros. *Alternatively, it could be labelled €/$, indicating that the axis shows the number of euros per dollar. If you use a fraction like this, the currency the graph is illustrating should always be in the denominator, or below the line in the fraction.*

III. Exchange Rate Determination

A. Floating Exchange Rate Systems. A floating exchange rate system is one in which the equilibrium exchange rate is determined solely by the free market supply of and demand for the currency. Therefore, anything that leads to a change in the demand for or supply of a currency will lead to a new equilibrium exchange rate.

1. Determinants of Demand for and Supply of a Currency

   i. Tastes and Preferences. As international consumers' tastes and preferences shift toward output produced in different countries, demand for different currencies rises and falls, affecting floating exchange rates.

      ➤ Assume Japanese cars become increasingly popular in Europe. The demand for Japanese yen will increase, and the supply of euros will increase, appreciating the yen and depreciating the euro.

      ➤ On the other hand, if Japanese airlines demand a large number of airplanes built in Europe, the demand for euros rises and supply of yen increases, appreciating the euro and depreciating the yen.

➤ In sum: As a nation's goods become more popular, its currency is likely to appreciate.

ii. Relative Income Levels. As the incomes of consumers abroad rise relative to domestic consumers, demand for the domestic currency increases because foreigners demand more imported goods. On the other hand, if foreign incomes fall relative to domestic incomes, demand for the domestic currency will decrease as foreigners desire to trade away less of their currencies for the domestic currency.

iii. Relative Inflation Rates. In a global economy, consumers base their buying decisions at least partially on where things are cheapest.

➤ If inflation is higher in one country than in a trading nation, the demand for the other country's currency will increase as consumers will wish to by the relatively cheaper imported goods.

➤ On the other hand, if inflation is lower in one country than others, then the demand for foreign currencies will decrease in the low-inflation country as consumers demand more domestically produced goods.

➤ In sum: A comparatively low price level or inflation rate will likely lead to appreciation of a country's currency.

iv. Relative Interest Rates. Interest rates determine the return on savings and other holdings such as bonds in various countries.

➤ If one country offers higher interest rates on savings relative to its trading partners, the demand for that country's currency rises, appreciating the currency.

➤ If a country lowers its interest rates relative to its trading partners, demand for its currency will fall since international investors will demand fewer of that country's assets, causing its currency to depreciate.

➤ In sum: Relative interest rates determine the flow of financial capital between nations. Capital tends to flow toward countries with higher interest rates, appreciating their currencies relative to those in countries with lower interest rates.

v. Speculation. The expectation of changes in a country's exchange rate among speculative investors may affect its exchange rate.

➤ If foreign investors expect a country's currency to appreciate, they will likely demand more of it now to hold onto as an asset until it is worth more, before trading it back for their own currency at a higher rate than that at which it was bought.

➤ On the other hand, if a currency is expected to depreciate, speculators will demand less of it and increase its supply, as they will not wish to be stuck holding the weaker currency in the future.

➤ In sum: Speculator expectations about changes in a currency's value become reality by leading to changes in the same direction as expected.

2. A change in any of the determinants of demand and supply for currencies will lead to a change in the equilibrium exchange rate between one currency and another.

i. The graph below identifies some of the possible causes of an appreciation of the euro and a depreciation of the yen.

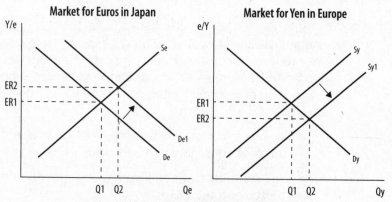

An appreciation of the euro and a depreciation of the yen could be caused by: (1) higher interest rates in Europe, (2) higher inflation in Japan, (3) higher incomes in Japan, (4) speculation that the euro will appreciate.

ii. The graph below shows some of the possible causes of a depreciation of the euro and an appreciation of the yen.

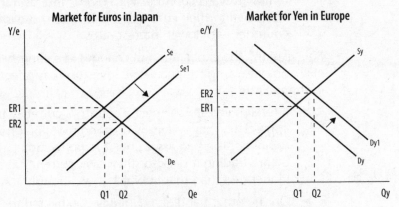

An appreciation of the yen and a depreciation of the euro could be caused by: (1) higher interest rates in Japan, (2) higher inflation in Europe, (3) higher incomes in Europe, (4) speculation that the yen will appreciate.

iii. In both the scenarios above, a change in one of the determinants of exchange rates causes one currency to appreciate and the other to depreciate.

B. Fixed and Managed Exchange Rate Systems. Sometimes governments will choose to manage its value or fix (peg) the value of its country's currency directly against another country's currency (usually a stable and internationally common currency like the US dollar or the British pound).

1. Managed exchange rates may be used for several reasons:

i. An artificially weak currency makes exports more attractive to foreign consumers, and imports less attractive to domestic consumers. A "devaluation" (a depreciation caused by government intervention) may be undertaken because

➤ A weaker currency will increase net exports and increase aggregate demand, and

➤ will contribute to employment and growth in domestic output, and

➤ will move a country's current account balance toward surplus.

ii. An artificially strong currency makes imported goods cheaper to domestic consumers and domestically produced goods more expensive to foreigners. A "revaluation" (an appreciation caused by government intervention) of its currency allows a government to reduce net exports and may be undertaken if

➤ a developing country wishes to acquire capital goods produced in more developed countries at lower costs, or

➤ a country is experiencing high inflation and needs to bring down aggregate demand to reduce inflation, or

➤ if a country wishes to reduce a large current account surplus.

2. Direct Intervention Using Foreign Exchange Reserves. A government may intervene directly in the market for its own currency or for the currency of the nation it wishes to manage its exchange rate against by buying or selling currency on the forex market.

i. Assume Brazil wishes to devalue its currency, the real, against the US dollar. In the forex diagram below, the equilibrium value of the real is $0.60. Brazil's government wishes to lower the exchange rate to $0.50.

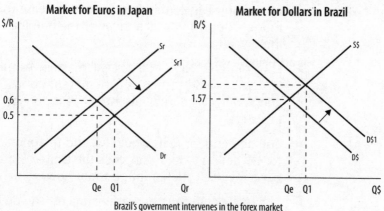

Brazil's government intervenes in the forex market
to devalue the real against the dollar.

➤ To accomplish this devaluation, the Brazilian government will buy dollars with reals (supplying reals in order to demand dollars).

➤ In the graph on the bottom left of page 263, the Brazilian government has increased the supply of real in the forex market, devaluing the real against the dollar.

➤ In the graph on the bottom right of page 263, Brazil's exchange of real for dollars increases the demand for dollars, causing the dollar to appreciate against the real.

➤ The weaker real will make Brazilian exports more attractive in the United States, increasing Brazil's net exports and contributing to aggregate demand.

3. Indirect Intervention Through Monetary Policy

   i. A primary determinant of the exchange rate between one country's currency and another's is the relative interest rates between the two countries.

   ii. If Brazil wishes to devalue its currency against the dollar, it can undertake a monetary policy that reduces interest rates on Brazilian investments.

➤ An open-market purchase of government bonds by the Brazilian central bank would increase the money supply in Brazil and lower the nominal interest rate.

➤ Lower interest rates in Brazil will make investments in Brazilian assets (such as government bonds and savings accounts) less attractive to foreign investors.

➤ The demand for reals would fall and the demand for US dollars would rise (since the United States has a relatively higher interest rate now).

➤ The real would then depreciate against the dollar, making Brazil's exports cheaper, increasing aggregate demand in Brazil.

iii. If a government or central bank wished to revalue (appreciate) its currency, it could reduce the money supply domestically, increasing the nominal interest rate and increasing capital inflows and the international demand for its currency, causing it to appreciate.

iv. Changes in a country's money market will lead to changes in its currency's demand in the forex market, as seen below.

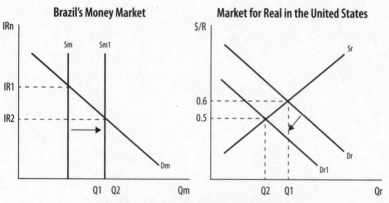

Brazil's domestic monetary policy affects demand for the real and the international value of the real.

➤ Expansionary monetary policy in Brazil increases the supply of money, reducing the domestic interest rate.

➤ Lower returns on investments in Brazil lead to a decrease in demand for the real on forex markets.

➤ The international value of the real falls against other currencies, such as the US dollar.

➤ A contractionary monetary policy in Brazil would have the opposite affect, increasing demand for the real and leading to its appreciation.

Questions about fixed exchange rates are rare, but those about managed or floating exchange rates are more common. Become familiar with the tools available to a central bank or government for managing the value of its exchange rate, and be able to illustrate the effects of such tools in the foreign exchange market diagram.

PART IX

TEST-TAKING STRATEGIES

Strategies for the
Multiple-Choice Questions

Each year the AP Macro exam starts with a 60-question multiple-choice section, which accounts for two-thirds (66.7 percent) of the final AP grade. Each question is worth one point, for a total of 60 points. There is **no penalty** for incorrect answers anymore, so there is no longer a reason *not to guess* if you are running out of time and have not finished all 60 questions or encounter a question that you cannot figure out.

Every year the multiple choice tends to follow a similar pattern in the order of questions. About ten questions are on topics from Unit 1—Basic Economic Concepts. This includes questions on opportunity cost, production possibilities, scarcity, the basic economic problem and economic resources, and basic supply and demand questions. The other fifty questions of the multiple-choice section venture into the realm of macro-specific material, covering topics from Units 2–7.

Typically, questions on open economy and international trade appear late in the exam, just as they appear late in the syllabus. Don't let the order of the questions concern you too much, however. What is most important is the number of questions that are likely to appear on each topic from the syllabus. The College Board publishes the approximate percentage of the multiple-choice questions covering each unit, and this information can be found in Chapter 1 of this Crash Course.

USE OF TIME ON THE MULTIPLE-CHOICE SECTION

You will have 70 minutes to answer the 60 multiple-choice questions, meaning that on average, you have 76 seconds per question. Don't interpret this fact to mean that you *should take* 76 seconds to answer each question. Some questions can be answered in far less than 76 seconds, while others will require more time to answer. Pacing yourself is important. If 35 minutes in the multiple-choice section have elapsed and you have not answered 30 questions, you are moving too slowly and may need to pick up the pace.

How do you know how much time to spend on certain questions? The trick is identifying what *knowledge* and what *skills* the question is assessing. Some questions test only basic knowledge from one section of the syllabus. Others test basic *skills*, while requiring only one piece of knowledge. On the other hand, some questions require knowledge of several sections of the syllabus and one or two skills to answer correctly. The relative complexity of the question should determine how much time you spend on a question. Less-complex questions require less time, while those requiring more skills and knowledge should consume the most time, naturally.

LEVEL 1 QUESTIONS—DEFINITIONAL

You can expect approximately 10 to 20 of the multiple-choice questions to be what can be described as Level 1 questions. These are the easiest and the quickest to answer, because they require only one piece of knowledge or one skill.

Example 1: The unemployment rate measures the percentage of

    (A) people in the labor force who do not have jobs

    (B) people in the labor force who have a part-time job but are looking for a full-time job

    (C) people who do not have jobs and have given up looking for work

    (D) people in the adult population who do not have jobs

    (E) people in the adult population who have temporary jobs

Most Level 1 questions are *definitional* in nature, which means they are basically testing to see if you know the definition of one of the terms from the syllabus. In the example above, the definition of "unemployment rate" is being tested. If you are familiar with this definition, answering this question should take almost no time at all. The unemployment rate measures the percentage of people in the labor force who do not have jobs. Therefore, (A) is the correct answer.

OTHER EXAMPLES OF LEVEL 1 QUESTIONS

In each of the examples that follow, one basic piece of knowledge or one basic skill is being tested. These questions should be the quickest and easiest to answer in the multiple-choice section. Therefore, no more than 20 to 30 seconds should be required.

Example 2: The sum of which of the following expenditures is equal to the value of the gross domestic product?

(A) Consumer purchases, investment for capital goods, exports, and imports

(B) Consumer purchases, investment for capital goods, net exports, and inventories

(C) Consumer purchases, investment for capital goods, government purchases, and net exports

(D) Consumer purchases, government purchases, exports, and national income

(E) Investment for capital goods, government purchases, net exports, and inventories

Example 3: A worker is cyclically unemployed if

(A) he has lost his job at a factory that has moved overseas.

(B) he is unable to find work because of a decrease in overall demand in the economy for goods and services.

(C) he is out of work because the hotel that employed him closed for the off-season.

(D) his skills are no longer needed in the economy.

(E) foreigners now do his job more efficiently than he does.

LEVEL 2 QUESTIONS—ANALYTICAL

The next level of difficulty on the multiple-choice section requires you to apply more than one skill or piece of knowledge to come to a correct answer. Analytical questions are the most common in the multiple-choice section, and will likely make up more than half of the 60 questions in total. These questions usually require a second step in the process of solving them. In addition to knowing a definition or a piece of knowledge, you may also be required to complete a calculation.

Example 1: Assume that the reserve requirement is 20 percent. If a bank initially has no excess reserves and $10,000 cash is deposited in the bank, the maximum amount by which this bank may increase its loans is

    (A) $2,000

    (B) $8,000

    (C) $10,000

    (D) $20,000

    (E) $50,000

The above question tests whether or not you know what is meant by "reserve requirement" and also whether or not you know how to measure the change in a bank's excess reserves following a change in checkable deposits. If you know that 80 percent of the $10,000 can be loaned out (since 20 percent must be kept on reserve), then you should be able to determine that the correct answer is (B).

OTHER EXAMPLES OF LEVEL 2 QUESTIONS

The questions below both require more than one thought process to solve. In each, a calculation or application of a skill learned in the course must be combined with one or more pieces of knowledge to come to a correct answer.

Example 2: Which of the following will necessarily result in a decrease in output?

I.   A rightward shift of the aggregate demand curve

II. A leftward shift of the aggregate demand curve

III. A rightward shift of the aggregate supply curve

IV. A leftward shift of the aggregate supply curve

(A) I only

(B) III only

(C) I and III only

(D) II and III only

(E) II and IV only

Example 3: Answer the following question on the basis of this information about a hypothetical economy:

Full-time employed = 750

Part-time employed = 200

Unemployed = 50

Discouraged workers = 50

Refer to the above information. The official unemployment rate is approximately

(A) 10 percent

(B) 30 percent

(C) 5 percent

(D) 7 percent

(E) 25 percent

LEVEL 3 QUESTIONS—SYNTHESIS

To synthesize means to pull your knowledge of several different topics together in order to answer a question. The most difficult and time-consuming questions in the multiple-choice section require this skill. You can expect between 10 and 20 questions to require synthesis. These questions will require the most time to answer, in some cases more than two minutes if multiple calculations or thought processes are needed. For synthesis questions, sketching quick graphs or solving simple math equations by taking scratch notes in the margin is highly advised.

Example 1: Under which of the following circumstances would increasing the money supply be most effective in increasing real gross domestic product?

	Interest Rates	Employment	Business Optimism
A.	High	Full	High
B.	High	Less than full	High
C.	High	Less than full	Low
D.	Low	Full	Low
E.	Low	Less than full	Low

On the surface, this question appears to be simply about monetary policy. But when looked at closely, it is not even asking a simple question such as, *"Which open market operation would a central bank use to lower interest rates?"* Rather, it is asking about the macroeconomic conditions under which expansionary monetary policy would be most effective.

This question requires that you pull together your knowledge from several parts of the syllabus. For example, you need to know that when interest rates are already low, expansionary monetary policy will do little to stimulate aggregate demand, because if firms were going to invest, they would be doing it at the already low interest rates. Just this knowledge helps you eliminate options (D) and (E).

Next you would need to consider the level of employment at the time the monetary policy is implemented. Consider option (A): If an economy is already producing at its full-employment level and business optimism is high, an increase in the money supply may increase investment and aggregate demand. However, due to the tight labor markets and the lack of available resources, real gross domestic product will not increase by very much (remember, SRAS curve is nearly vertical beyond full employment), while inflation will increase rapidly. For this reason, we can eliminate option (A).

When considering option (C), we can eliminate it since whenever there is low business confidence, monetary policies will likely be ineffective, since lower interest rates will not be enough to encourage firms to invest.

Now consider option (B). If interest rates are high, then increasing the money supply should bring them down. If business optimism is high, the lower rates should stimulate new investment. Finally, if the economy is already producing at a level of output that is less than its full-employment level, then the economy has room to grow. The lower interest rates and high business optimism will encourage firms to invest in new capital equipment and hire unemployed workers, increasing the level of real gross domestic product while the price level remains fairly stable or increases only slightly. The correct answer, therefore, is option (B).

Clearly, the number of processes required to come to a correct answer of (B) is far greater than that required to answer a Level 1 or a Level 2 question because greater evaluation of various pieces of knowledge is involved. Therefore, Level 3 questions should take more time to answer than the other two types.

OTHER EXAMPLES OF LEVEL 3 QUESTIONS

The questions below require the synthesis or evaluation of various pieces of knowledge and skills from different part of the syllabus to answer. Therefore, they can both be considered Level 3 questions.

Example 2: Suppose that, from 1985 to 1986, unemployment fell from nine percent to five percent and inflation (the change in the price level) fell from four percent to one and one-half percent. An explanation of these changes might be that the

A. aggregate demand curve shifted to the left

B. aggregate demand curve shifted to the right

C. aggregate supply curve shifted to the left

D. aggregate supply curve shifted to the right

E. both aggregate demand and aggregate supply curves shifted to the left

Example 3: In a flexible system of exchange rates, an open-market sale of bonds by the Federal Reserve will most likely change the money supply, the interest rate, and the value of the United States dollar in which of the following ways?

	Money Supply	Interest Rate	Value of the Dollar
A.	Increase	Decrease	Decrease
B.	Increase	Decrease	Increase
C.	Decrease	Decrease	Decrease
D.	Decrease	Increase	Increase
E.	Decrease	Increase	Decrease

Tips from AP Macro students: The following are some other "rules of thumb" to keep in mind when approaching the multiple-choice section. Not all the points below are true in every case, but many could be helpful in guiding you to the correct answer.

➤ If you are sure that two answers are saying basically the same thing in different ways, neither one is probably the right answer, since they both can't be right.

➤ If two responses are opposites, it is likely but not definite that one of these is the correct choice. Look especially for situations in which you can find the one choice distinct from the other four.

➤ Answers may be clumped by similarity, three that are similar and two that are obviously different. Much of the time, the correct answer is one of the three that are similar. It would be unusual for the correct answer to be one of two that are similar, since the AP tends to give you more options that *sound like they could be correct* and then make you choose from one of those.

➤ You need to know definitions. Even though there won't be many questions that are strictly definitional, knowing definitions is necessary to answer more of the complicated questions as well. Plus, the definitional questions are supposed to be the easiest ones, so you might as well aim to get those right.

➤ Use practice tests to study. If your teacher does not provide you with practice exams, consider buying a review book that includes AP-style practice questions with good explanations teaching you why the wrong answers are wrong. Remember also that the website for this book includes a practice exam you can take (*http://www.rea.com/studycenter*).

➤ When taking practice tests, identify the answers you got wrong, look for trends, and go back and study those topics specifically. Focusing your time studying the concepts you are weakest in is better than trying to study every concept in the course equally.

➤ Never choose a multiple-choice answer without reading all the other options first. You may think you've read the right answer, but may discover that another option is even better.

➤ Cross off answers that you *know* are wrong. This will help you narrow down the possibilities to the best answer, and prevent you from re-reading answers you have already read and discounted as a possibility.

➤ Some of the hardest multiple-choice questions ask about relatively simple concepts but in new or seemingly confusing phrasing. Look for ways to simplify the text in the questions or consider alternate meanings of words so you can make a better guess.

Strategies for the Free-Response Questions

After completing the 60-question multiple-choice section, you will have a short break before returning to begin the 60-minute FRQ section. FRQ stands for free-response questions. Don't be fooled, though, because the responses you provide in this section are hardly expected to be "free." In fact, there are some pretty clear rules of thumb you can follow to ensure that your answers to these questions fulfill the graders' expectations as well as present your responses in a way that demonstrates a clear understanding of the concepts, thereby ensuring that you earn a top score.

The FRQ section of the exam is 60 minutes long and the first 10 minutes is a mandatory reading period. The remaining 50 minutes may be spent writing your responses to three questions. The three FRQs are always in the following format:

➤ Question 1—the long FRQ: This question is always the longest of the three FRQs, and usually includes more "parts" than questions 2 and 3. This question counts for half the FRQ score, so 5 of your 10 reading minutes and 25 of the 50 minutes you have to write in the FRQ section should be devoted to answering question 1.

➤ Questions 2 and 3—the short FRQs. The second and third questions on the FRQ section are always shorter and include fewer "parts" than question 1. Each of these questions is equally weighted and worth 25 percent of your FRQ score, so these should be given approximately 12.5 minutes each, or a total of 25 minutes between them, in addition to half of your planning and reading time.

The FRQ section can be your worst enemy or your best friend, depending on how well prepared you are going into it. The best way to be prepared is to have a good idea of what is most likely to appear in each of three FRQs, and to have completed as many practice FRQs as you can get your hands on. Fortunately for you, the AP releases all of its past FRQs to students, *with scoring guides*, for free download on its Student Resource page online. This site should be bookmarked in your browser and visited before every unit test your teacher gives you: *http://www.collegeboard.org*.

WHICH TOPICS WILL THE FRQs COVER?

While technically the topics covered in each FRQ can come from any section of the syllabus, there are topics that seem to be tested more commonly in each of the three questions, lending some predictability to the makeup of the FRQ section.

The table below shows the topics tested over each of the last three years in the FRQ section. Notice first of all that there are two FRQ exams released each year, and one is called "Form B." This exam is the one given to international students, while the "regular" exam is the one taken by students in the United States. The three columns on the right of the table identify the concepts tested in each of three FRQs from each year's exam.

Exam	FRQ #1	FRQ #2	FRQ #3
2011	Phillips Curve (SR and LR), AD/AS, fiscal policy, OMO, money market, SR to LR in AD/AS	Loanable funds market, investment demand and real interest rates, forex market, determinant of exchange rates	RRR, OMO, money multiplier, bond market
2011 Form B	AD/AS, determinants of AD, Phillips Curve (SR and LR), automatic fiscal policy, loanable funds market with crowding-out SR to LR in the AD/AS model	Forex markets, impact of exchange rates on AD/AS, monetary policy's effects on exchange rates	Calculating GDP, nominal and real, price indexes, nominal and real wages, nominal and real interest rates

Exam	FRQ #1	FRQ #2	FRQ #3
2010	AD/AS, fiscal policy, SR to LR in AD/AS, loanable funds market with crowding out, investment demand	Money market, money demand, bond market, OMO	Forex markets, impact of exchange rates on AD/AS, determinants of exchange rates
2010 Form B	AD/AS, fiscal policy, SR Phillips Curve, crowding out, PPC	OMO, money market, effect of monetary policy on exchange rates	Determinants of AD/AS, impact of various supply and demand shocks
2009	Phillips Curve (SR/LR), OMO, money market, AD/AS	Forex market, loanable funds market, determinants of exchange rates	RRR, money multiplier, OMO
2009 Form B	AD/AS, short-run Phillips Curve, fiscal policy, SR to LR in AD/AS	RRR, OMO, money multiplier, money market, effects of inflation	Forex market, determinants of exchange rates, loanable funds market

From the table above, you can see that FRQ #1 always requires students to draw an AD/AS diagram. Other topics and graphs that commonly appear in FRQ #1 are:

➤ Short-run and long-run effects of changes to AD or AS;

➤ Movements along and shifts in the Phillips Curve, both short run and long run;

➤ A money market diagram illustrating the effect of a monetary policy action;

➤ A loanable funds diagram illustrating the crowding-out effect of a fiscal policy action;

➤ On rare occasions, a forex market showing an appreciation or depreciation of a country's currency.

FRQs #2 and #3 generally cover a range of topics from the syllabus, some of the most common of which include:

➤ exchange rates, forex markets, and determinants of exchange rates;

➤ the effect of a change in deposits in the banking system, using the money multiplier;

➤ causes and effects of changes to the nominal and real interest rates illustrated in the money market and the loanable funds market;

➤ money market showing the effect of a monetary policy action;

➤ occasionally a Phillips Curve diagram showing the trade-off between inflation and unemployment.

For a list of the question-by-question FRQ topics going back to 1999, check out the author of this book's website, where he has posted a table of past Macro FRQ topics: *http://welkerswikinomics.com*.

THE STRUCTURE OF AN FRQ

Free-response questions follow a fairly standard structure. They always include multiple "parts" (a, b, c, etc.) and almost always require you to draw a graph. The standard prompts on an FRQ are the following:

SHOW:

FRQ #1 always requires at least one, usually more than one, diagrams *showing* some macroeconomic effect. Questions that ask you to *show* something are usually accompanied by the words *"Using a _____ diagram,"* in which the blank would tell you which diagram to use. Sometimes, however, it will say, *"Using an appropriate diagram, show . . ."* In such a case, it is up to you to decide which diagram to use.

A question asking you to show something will be worth at least two points. One for showing the correct effect, another for drawing a correctly labeled diagram. Depending on the complexity of the diagram required, such a question may be worth as many as three or four points. Even if you are confused about how to show an effect, you can often earn some or most of the points by labeling an appropriate diagram.

IDENTIFY:

Identification questions should be the easiest to answer. They may not actually use the word "identify," but may ask you to identify indirectly by asking how something will change. For example: *"How will the higher real interest rate affect aggregate demand?"* or *"Indicate what will happen to the unemployment rate in the short run as output declines."* In such a question, all that is expected of you is to identify the result of something happening. In this case, *AD would decrease* or *the unemployment rate would rise.* Such a response would earn you one point, which is all such a question would be worth.

Unless the question explicitly asks for an explanation, it is not necessary for you to provide one. Having a good explanation in mind when you form your answer, however, is advisable since it increases the odds that you will have the right response.

CALCULATE:

Calculations require you to apply one of the formulas you learned in class. Some of the things you may be called upon to calculate are:

➤ nominal GDP from a set of data;

➤ a price index from a set of data;

➤ the inflation rate from a set of data;

➤ the change in GDP that will result from a particular fiscal policy (using the spending multiplier), or the size of a change in spending needed to bring about a particular change in GDP;

➤ a change in the money supply following a change in checkable deposits or following an open-market operation by the Fed;

➤ a change in a bank's required or excess reserves following a change in checkable deposits or an open-market operation by the Fed;

➤ the real interest rate using nominal interest rate and inflation data;

➤ the opportunity cost of one good in terms of another.

Calculation problems are generally only worth one point each. If you get the calculation right, you score the point. If you get it wrong, the point is subtracted from your final score. Sometimes you will be asked to show the work you used in the calculation.

Correctly solving calculation problems is a skill that can be perfected through practice. To prepare for these questions, you should become familiar with all of the calculations identified above and complete as many past FRQs as possible to become familiar with the type of calculation that appears in the FRQ section.

Remember, calculators are not allowed on the AP Macro exam, so all calculations must be done from scratch with pen and paper. Fortunately for you, this also means that the test creators cannot expect you to handle really nasty numbers. So, if you get a calculation that seems messy, it may be a useful indication that you set the problem up wrong.

EXPLAIN:

Explanations are not always required to earn the points on one part of an FRQ. But sometimes they are, and if they are, the question will make it perfectly clear that an explanation is expected. Study the following two examples and determine the difference between them:

➤ Example 1: "How will the change in the interest rate you identified in part (b) affect aggregate demand?"

➤ Example 2: "Explain how the change in the interest rate you identified in part (b) will affect aggregate demand."

At first glance, there may appear to be no difference between these two questions. However, example 1 is only a one-point question, while example 2 is worth at least two points. Here's why:

➤ The first example is an *identify* question. It is basically asking you to identify how a change in interest rates affects aggregate demand. A correct answer would be that AD either increased, decreased, or stayed the same. No explanation is needed for example 1.

➤ Example 2 asks you to *explain* how a change in the interest rate affects aggregate demand. To earn the two (or more) points this question is worth, you would need to not only indicate how AD changes, but also offer an explanation. Assume in part (b) you indicated that interest rates increased. A suitable answer to this question would then be:

"The increase in interest rates will increase borrowing costs for firms, which will lead to less investment, reducing the level of aggregate demand in the economy."

This response clearly explains *why* AD decreases, whereas for example 1 a simple *"AD decreases"* would have been suitable.

TIPS FROM AP MACRO STUDENTS

This chapter has attempted to demystify the free-response section of the AP Macroeconomics exam. While this section may be intimidating at first, it is actually the easiest to prepare for and to succeed in if you know what you're getting into. Below are some final student tips for how to succeed on the FRQ section:

➤ If a question does not say "explain," don't attempt an explanation.

➤ Look for the key words "identify," "show," and "explain," and do exactly what the question asks you to do.

➤ Study past FRQs on the College Board's AP Macro student page. Use the scoring guidelines and become familiar with how they are graded.

➤ Master the graphs. Much of your FRQ grade depends on the quality and accuracy of the diagrams you draw. Correctly labeling graphs and drawing them large and with great detail is the best way to ensure you will earn easy points on the FRQs.

➤ Practice calculations. Almost every FRQ exam requires at least one calculation. Chapter 2 of this book includes a list of the formulas you need to know for the AP Macro course. Be familiar with these and know how to use them.

➤ Sometimes less is more. Keep in mind that AP exams are graded by real teachers, who will read thousands of FRQs in a week. Being wordy may harm you. Be concise and to the point, and try to say things in as few words as necessary.

➤ Plan more to write less. The 10 minutes of reading time is not enough to ingest all that is going on in all three questions. On the other hand, it takes far less than 50 minutes to craft neatly in the answer book the responses necessary to earn all the credit on all the questions. Some students use as much as 20 or even 30 minutes of the 60-minute period reading, analyzing, and recording rough responses to all three questions in the question folder and only half or a bit more of their time copying these graphs and explanations into the pink response book. Practice will guide you as to the correct allocation of time.

➤ No tricks. FRQs tend to be straightforward and not subject to nuanced differences of interpretation. It is far more common that a single multiple-choice question will be a "trick question."

➤ Use context. Sometimes a part in the middle of an FRQ item will challenge you. Often there is a logical flow of all the parts to a question, and you can use this to your advantage. Consider what was asked prior and what is asked after the item troubling you and you may see the middle appear in your mind.

Economics Glossary

Aggregate demand—shows the total quantity of goods and services consumed at different price and output levels.

Aggregate demand/aggregate supply (AD/AS) model—uses aggregate demand and aggregate supply to determine and explain price level, real domestic output, disposable income, and employment.

Aggregate expenditure—all spending for final goods and services in an economy: $C + I_g + G + Xn = AE$.

Allocative efficiency—distribution of resources among firms and industries to obtain production quantities of the products most wanted by society (consumers); where marginal cost equals marginal benefit.

Appreciation (of the dollar)—an increase in the value of the dollar relative to the currency of another nation, so that a dollar buys more of the foreign currency and thus foreign goods become cheaper; critical to long-run trade equilibrium.

Asset—items of monetary value owned by a firm or individual; opposite is *liability*.

Average fixed cost (AFC)—firm's total fixed cost divided by output.

Average product—total output produced per unit of a resource employed (total product divided by the quantity of input).

Average total cost (ATC)—firm's total cost divided by output, equal to average fixed cost plus average variable cost (AFC + AVC = ATC).

Average variable cost (AVC)—firm's total variable cost divided by output.

Balance of payments account—summary of a nation's current account and its financial account.

Balance of trade—a nation's current account balance; net exports.

Balance sheet—statement of the assets and liabilities that determines a firm's net (solvency).

Barrier to entry—artificial prevention of the entry of firms into an industry.

Bond—financial instrument through which a borrower (corporate or government) is contracted to pay the principal at a specified interest rate at a specific date (maturity) in the future; promissory note.

Breakeven point—output at which a (competitive) firm's total cost and total revenue are equal (TR = TC); an output at which a firm has neither an economic profit nor a loss, at which it earns only a normal profit.

Budget deficit—amount by which the spending of the (federal) government exceeds its tax revenues in any year.

Budget surplus—amount by which the tax revenues of the (federal) government exceed its spending in any year.

Capital—resources (buildings, machinery, and equipment) used to produce goods and services; also called *investment goods*.

Capital account—section of a nation's international balance-of-payments balance sheet that records foreign purchases of U.S. assets (money in) and U.S. purchases of foreign assets (money out).

Capital account inflow (outflow)—reflects the net difference between foreign funds invested in the home country minus the domestic funds invested in the foreign country; component of the balance of payments account.

Capitalism—free market economic system in which property is privately owned and the invisible forces of supply and demand set price and quantity.

Cartel—overt agreement among firms (or countries) in an industry to fix the price of a product and establish output quotas.

Change in demand—change in the quantity demanded of a good or service at all prices; a shift of the demand curve to the left (decrease) or right (increase).

Change in supply—change in the quantity supplied of a good or service at all prices; a shift of the supply curve to the left (decrease) or right (increase).

Circular flow model—flow of resource inputs from households to businesses and of goods and services (g/s) from businesses to households. A flow in the opposite direction of money—businesses to households for inputs and from households to businesses for g/s—occurs simultaneously.

Comparative advantage—determines specialization and exchange rate for trade between nations; based on the nation with the lower relative or comparative cost of production.

Competition—Adam Smith's requirement for success of a free market, a market of independent buyers and sellers competing with one another; includes ease of access to and exit from the marketplace.

Complementary goods—goods that are used together, so if the price of one falls, the demand for the other decreases as well (and vice versa).

Consumer price index (CPI)—index that measures the prices of a set "basket" of some 300 goods and services bought by a "typical" consumer; used by government as a main indicator of the rate of inflation.

Consumer surplus—that portion of the demand curve that lies above the equilibrium price level and denotes those consumers that would be willing to buy the goods and services at higher price levels.

Contractionary fiscal policy—combination of government reduction in spending and a net increase in taxes, for the purpose of decreasing aggregate demand, lowering price levels, and thus controlling inflation.

Corporation—legal entity ("like a person") chartered by a state or the federal government; limits liability for business debt to the assets of the firm.

Cost-push inflation—when an increase in resource costs shifts the aggregate supply curve inward, resulting in an increase in the price level and unemployment; also termed *stagflation*.

Cross elasticity of demand—ratio of the percentage change in quantity demanded of one good to the percentage change in the price of another good. If the coefficient is positive, the two goods are substitute. If the coefficient is negative, they are considered complementary.

Crowding-out effect—caused by the federal government's increased borrowing in the money market that results in a rise in interest rates. The rise in interest rates results in a decrease in gross business domestic investment (I_g), which reduces the effectiveness of expansionary fiscal policy.

Current account—section in a nation's international balance of payments that records its exports and imports of goods and services, its net investment income, and its net transfers; component of the balance of payments account.

Cyclical deficit—government budget deficit caused by a recession and the resultant decline in tax revenues.

Cyclical unemployment—type of unemployment caused by recession; less than full employment aggregate demand.

Deadweight loss (efficiency loss)—the foregone total societal surplus associated with the levy of a tax that discourages what had heretofore been a mutually advantageous market transaction.

Deflation—decline in the economy's price level; indicates contraction in business cycle or may signal expansion of total output (aggregate supply moves to the right).

Demand—the quantity of a good or service that buyers wish to buy at various prices.

Depreciation (of the dollar)—decrease in the value of the dollar relative to another currency, so that the dollar buys a smaller amount of the foreign currency and therefore the price of foreign goods increases; tends to reduce imports and increase exports.

Determinants of demand—factors other than price that alter (shift) the quantities demanded of a good or service.

Determinants of supply—factors other than price that alter (shift) the quantities supplied of a good or service.

Discount rate—interest rate that the Federal Reserve Banks charge on the loans they make to banks (different from the federal funds rate).

Disposable income—personal income minus personal taxes; income available for consumption expenditures and saving.

Durable good—consumer good with an expected life (use) of three or more years; decrease in sales indicates recession, as contraction affects these goods before nondurables.

Economic efficiency—use of the minimum necessary inputs to obtain the most societally beneficial quantity of goods and services; employs both productive and allocative efficiency.

Economic profit—total revenue of a firm minus its economic costs (both explicit and implicit costs); also termed *pure profit* and *above-normal profit*.

Economies of scale—savings in the average total cost of production as the firm expands the size of plant (its output) in the long run.

Elastic demand—product or resource demand whose price elasticity is greater than 1. This means that the resulting percentage change in quantity demanded is greater than the percentage change in price.

Elastic supply—product or resource supply whose price elasticity is greater than 1. This means that the resulting percentage change in quantity supplied is greater than the percentage change in price.

Equilibrium price—price at which the quantity demanded and the quantity supplied are equal (intersect), shelves clear, and price stability occurs.

Equilibrium quantity—quantity demanded and supplied at the equilibrium price.

Excess capacity—plant resources underused when imperfectly competitive firms produce less output than that associated with achieving minimum average total cost.

Expansionary fiscal policy—combination of government increases in spending and a net decrease in taxes, for the purpose of increasing aggregate demand, increasing output and disposable income, and lowering unemployment.

Expected rate of return—profit a firm anticipates it will obtain by purchasing capital goods; influences investment demand for money.

Factors of production—resources: land, capital, and entrepreneurial ability.

Federal funds rate—the interest rate banks and other depository institutions charge one another on overnight loans made out of their excess reserves; targeted by monetary policy.

Financial account (capital account)—the difference between a country's sale of assets to foreigners and its purchase of foreign assets; component of the balance of payments account.

Fixed cost—any cost that remains constant when the firm changes its output.

Fixed exchange rate—rate of currency exchange that is set, prevented from rising or falling with changes in currency supply and demand; opposite of floating exchange rate.

Frictional unemployment—unemployment caused by workers' voluntarily changing jobs or workers' being between jobs.

Full employment unemployment rate—natural rate of unemployment when there is no cyclical unemployment. In the United States, it equals between 4 percent and 5 percent, because some frictional and structural unemployment is unavoidable.

Gross domestic product (GDP)—total market value of all final goods and services produced annually within the boundaries of the United States, whether by U.S. or foreign-supplied resources.

Horizontal merger—merger into a single firm of two firms that produce the same product and sell it in the same geographic market.

Hyperinflation—a very rapid rise in the price level; an extremely high rate of inflation.

Imperfect competition—all market structures except pure competition; includes monopoly, monopolistic competition, and oligopoly.

Implicit cost—the monetary income a firm sacrifices when it uses a resource it owns rather than supplying the resource in the market; equal to what the resource could have earned in the best-paying alternative employment; includes a normal profit.

Indifference curve—curve showing the different combinations of two products that yield the same satisfaction or utility to a consumer.

Inelastic demand—product or resource demand for which the elasticity coefficient for price is less than 1. This means the resulting percentage change in quantity demanded is less than the percentage change in price.

Inelastic supply—product or resource supply for which the price elasticity coefficient is less than 1. The percentage change in quantity supplied is less than the percentage change in price.

Inferior good—a good or service the consumption of which declines as income rises (and vice versa), with price remaining constant.

Inflation—rise in the general level of prices.

Inflation (rational) expectation—a key determinant that impacts the loanable funds market for both borrowers and lenders.

Inflationary gap—amount by which the aggregate expenditure and schedule must shift downward to decrease the nominal gross domestic product (GDP) to its full employment noninflationary level.

Interest—payment for the use of borrowed money.

Inventories—goods that have been produced but remain unsold.

Inverse relationship—the relationship between two variables that change in opposite directions; for example, product price and quantity demanded.

Kinked demand curve—demand curve for a noncollusive oligopolist, which is based on the assumption that rivals will follow a price decrease and ignore a price increase.

Law of demand—the principle that, other things being equal, an increase in the price of a product will reduce the quantity of that product demanded, and conversely for a decrease in price.

Law of diminishing marginal utility—the principle that as a consumer increases the consumption of a good or service (g/s), the marginal utility obtained from each additional unit of the g/s decreases.

Law of diminishing returns—the principle that as successive increments of a variable resource are added to a fixed resource, the marginal product of the variable resource will eventually decrease.

Law of increasing opportunity costs—the principle that as the production of a good increases, the opportunity cost of producing an additional unit rises.

Law of supply—the principle that, other things being equal, an increase in the price of a product will increase the quantity of that product supplied, and conversely for a price decrease.

Liability—a debt with a monetary value; an amount owed by a firm or an individual.

Liquidity—the ease with which an asset can be converted—quickly—into cash with little or no loss of purchasing power. Money is said to be perfectly liquid, whereas other assets have a lesser degree of liquidity.

Loanable funds market—a conceptual market wherein the demand for money is determined by borrowers and the supply is determined by lenders. Market equilibrium prices the interest rate.

Long run—time frame necessary for producers to alter resource inputs and increase or decrease output; time frame necessary for adjustments to be made as a result of shifts in aggregate demand and supply.

Lorenz curve—a model that demonstrates the cumulative percentage of population and their cumulative share of income; used to show shifts in income distribution across population over time.

M_1, M_2, M_3—money supply measurements that increasingly broaden the definition of money measured; critical to monetarism and interest rates.

Macroeconomics—the portion of economics concerned with the overall performance of the economy; focused on aggregate demand–aggregate supply relationship, and the resultant output, income, employment, and price levels.

Marginal benefit—change in total benefit that results from the consumption of one more unit of output.

Marginal cost—change in total cost that results from the sale of one more unit of output.

Marginal product—change in total output relative to the change in resource input.

Marginal propensity to consume—change in consumption spending relative to a change in income.

Marginal propensity to save—change in saving relative to a change in income.

Marginal revenue—change in total revenue that results from the sale of one more unit of product.

Marginal revenue cost (MRC)—change in total cost with the addition of one more unit of resource input for production.

Marginal revenue product (MRP)—change in total revenue with the addition of one more unit of resource input for production.

Marginal utility—the use a consumer gains from the addition of one more unit of a good or service.

Market failure—the inability of the free market to provide public goods; over- or underallocation of goods or services that have negative/positive externalities; used to justify government intervention.

Microeconomics—portion of economics concerned with the individual elements that make up the economy: households, firms, government, and resource input prices.

Monetary policy—policy basis on which the Federal Reserve influences interest rates through manipulation of the money supply to promote price stability, full employment, and productivity growth.

Money—any article (paper note, metal coin) generally accepted as having value in exchange for a good or service.

Money supply—defined, measured, and reported as M_1, M_2, M_3.

Monopsony—a market structure in which there is only one buyer of a resource input or good or service.

MR = MC principle—law stating that to maximize profit and minimize loss, a firm will produce at the output level where the marginal revenue is equal to the marginal cost.

MRP = MRC formula—equation showing that to maximize profit and minimize loss, a firm will employ a resource input quantity when the marginal revenue product is equal to the marginal resource cost of the resource input.

Multiplier—the effect that a change in one of the four components of aggregate expenditure has on gross domestic product (GDP).

Natural monopoly—an industry in which the economy of scale is so large that one producer is the most efficient least-cost producer; usually regulated by government.

Natural rate of unemployment—frictional and structural unemployment, the full employment rate, zero cyclical unemployment.

Net export effect—any monetary or fiscal policy action is magnified (+ or –) by the effect that the change in U.S. dollar value (interest rates effect exchange rates) has on import and export prices.

Nominal—any economic measurement that is not adjusted for inflation.

Nominal interest rate—the interest rate that is not adjusted for inflation.

Normal good—a good or service (g/s) the consumption of which increases as income increases (opposite of inferior g/s).

Normal profit—where price equals average total cost, and cost includes the implicit cost of entrepreneurial value.

Oligopoly—a market structure in which a few firms have a large market share and sell differentiated products. In oligopolies, firms tend to have large economies of scale, pricing is mutually dependent, and price wars can occur; there is a kinked demand curve.

Perfectly elastic demand—infinite quantity demanded at a particular price; graphed as a straight horizontal line.

Perfectly elastic supply—infinite quantity supplied at a particular price; graphed as a straight horizontal line.

Perfectly inelastic demand—quantity demanded does not change in response to a change in price; graphed as a vertical straight line.

Perfectly inelastic supply—quantity supplied does not change in response to a change in price; graphed as a horizontal straight line.

Phillips curve (short run)—a model that demonstrates the inverse relationship between unemployment (horizontal) and inflation (vertical axis).

Phillips curve (long run)—a model demonstrating that, after inflation expectations have been adjusted for, there is no trade-off between inflation and unemployment because it is vertical and equal to the natural rate of unemployment.

Price—the sum of money necessary to purchase a good or service.

Price = MC—in a purely competitive market model, the principle that a firm's demand is perfectly elastic and equal to price, so that a firm will maximize profit when price equals marginal cost if price is equal to or greater than average total cost (ATC) and minimize loss if price is greater than average variable cost (AVC).

Price ceiling—a price set below equilibrium by government.

Price elasticity of demand—percentage of change in quantity demanded divided by percentage of change in price; measures responsiveness to price changes.

Price elasticity of supply—percentage of change in quantity supplied divided by percentage of change in price; measures responsiveness to price changes.

Price fixing—illegal collusion between producers to set an above-equilibrium price.

Price floor—a price set above equilibrium by government.

Producer surplus—that portion of the supply curve that lies below equilibrium price and denotes producers that would bring the goods or services to market at even lower prices.

Progressive tax—a marginal tax rate system in which the percentage of tax increases as income increases and vice versa (such as U.S. federal income tax brackets).

Proportional tax—a flat tax system in which the percentage of tax remains fixed as income changes.

Pure competition—market structure in which so many firms produce a very similar good or service that no firm has significant control over market price; a "price taker."

Pure monopoly—market structure in which one firm is the sole producer of a distinct good or service and thus has significant control over market price; a "price maker."

Quantity demanded—various amounts along a consumer demand curve showing the quantity consumers will buy at various prices.

Quantity supplied—various amounts along a producer supply curve showing the quantity producers will sell at various prices.

Recession—two consecutive business quarters of negative real gross domestic product (GDP).

Regressive tax—a set tax percentage the average rate of which decreases as the taxpayer's income increases, and vice versa; an example is sales tax.

Shortage—difference between the quantity demanded of a good or service and the quantity supplied at a below-equilibrium price ($Q_d > Q_s$).

Short run—the length of time during which a producer is unable to alter all the inputs of production.

Sole proprietorship—an unincorporated business owned by an individual.

Specialization—concentration of resource(s) in the production of a good or service that results in increased efficiency of production.

Stock—an ownership share in a company held by an investor.

Structural unemployment—unemployment resulting from a mismatch of worker skill to demand or location.

Substitute—goods or services that are interchangeable. When the price of one increases, the demand for the other increases.

Supply-side economics—macroeconomic perspective that emphasizes fiscal policies aimed at altering the state of the economy through I_g (short run) and the aggregate supply (long run).

Surplus—difference between the quantity demanded of a good or service and the quantity supplied at an above-equilibrium price ($Q_d < Q_s$).

Tariff—a tax on imports/exports.

Tax—a required payment of money to government, for which the payer receives no direct goods or services.

Trade deficit—amount by which a nation's imports exceed its exports.

Trade-off—forgone alternative use of a resource in the production of a good or service.

Trade surplus—amount by which a nation's exports exceed its imports.

Variable cost—cost of inputs that fluctuates as a firm increases or decreases its output.